W9-CYD-841

Negotiated Evaluation

Involving Children and Parents in the Process

Helen Woodward

HEINEMANN
Portsmouth, NH

To Dad, who always believed in me.

HEINEMANN
A division of Reed Elsevier Inc.
361 Hanover Street
Portsmouth, NH 03801-3912

Offices and agents throughout the world

First published 1993 by
Primary English Teaching Association
Laura Street
Newtown
NSW 2042
Australia

Library of Congress Cataloging-in-Publication Data

Woodward, Helen, 1939-
　　　Negotiated evaluation : involving children and parents in the
process / Helen Woodward.
　　　　　p.　　　cm.
　　　Includes bibliographical references.
　　　ISBN 0-435-08822-X (alk. paper) : $13.50
　　　1. Educational tests and measurements—Australia.　2. Education-
-Parent participation—Australia.　3. Language arts—Australia-
-Evaluation.　　　I. Title.
LB3058.A8W66　　1994
371.2'7'0994–dc20　　　　　　　　　　　　　　　　　94-27613
　　　　　　　　　　　　　　　　　　　　　　　　　　　CIP

Cover design by Jenny Jensen Greenleaf
Printed in the United States of America on acid-free paper
99　98　97　96　95　94　CC　1　2　3　4　5　6　7　8　9

Contents

Acknowledgements

I would like to express my gratitude to the following people:

Viv Nicoll, without whose support this book would never have eventuated;

Alison Preece, whose ideas, humour and friendship have constantly encouraged me, and her colleagues at the University of Victoria, British Columbia, for their support;

Sue Dockett and my colleagues at the University of Western Sydney, Macarthur, for their support and encouragement;

Jan Hancock for continually challenging my ideas and allowing me to be part of hers;

Stan Warren, Sue Edwards and the staff, children and parents at Nareena Hills Public School for their acceptance of my ideas and for their willingness to be part of an adventure;

Steve Orton, Ray McCauley and the staff, parents and children of Thomas Acres Public School for their diligence, their support and the energy expended in being at the forefront of educational change;

the many teachers who have helped me to develop my ideas, given me stories and extended my thinking — including Joy Paquin and Diane Cowden (Canada), Pat McLure (New Hampshire), Chris Gibson (St Paul of the Apostle School, Winston Hills), Robyn Hutchins and the teachers at St Bernadette's Primary School (Castle Hill), Graham Rayner (Scone Public School);

the many children who have been at the centre of this idea, and the parents who have supported the adventurers in this program;

my many friends who have shown me that an idea is but a beginning.

Introduction

'Excuse me, Ms Mahon, aren't you specially watching Emanuel this week?'
'Yes, Kari, I am.'
'Then he's just climbed up the ladder and right across the monkey bars.'
'Thank you, Kari.'
'Now have you got that written down, Ms Mahon?'

Such is the interest and enthusiasm of the children in a classroom where 'negotiated evaluation' is a normal part of the daily routine. The children understand and value the processes involved and are anxious to join in helping the teacher evaluate each child.

So what is negotiated evaluation? It is a system of evaluation which helps all those with a vested interest in a child's progress to make accurate decisions about that child in order to better accommodate and stimulate his or her learning, as well as to record and report the child's progress over time.

Some definitions

Over the years many different, often confusing definitions of assessment and evaluation have appeared in print. Some school systems see assessment as the collection of information and evaluation as the analysis of this information, while others see assessment as the collection of information about students and evaluation as the collection of information about programs, policies and procedures (for example, the Department of School Education in NSW defines assessment and evaluation in this way). Because I have difficulty in separating information about students from information about programs, I prefer to use the single word 'evaluation' to encompass all these concepts. I have chosen this term partly because it comes (through French) from the Latin *valere*, meaning to be strong/healthy/vigorous, and it is children's strengths I focus on as I evaluate them.

The definition of evaluation from which I have worked is this:

Evaluation is the collection and analysis of data, from a variety of sources and perspectives, which will contribute to:

- *making judgements of merit and worth*

- *making decisions about future planning*

- *informing learning.*

In order to ensure that our evaluation is trustworthy, we must collect data from a variety of contexts (i.e. from different experiences and situations) and from a variety of perspectives (i.e. from the viewpoints of different people). We must then analyse it to ascertain the quality of the learning processes and products involved — in other words, we must make judgements about their merit and worth. Having done this, we must ensure that we use the information we have gathered to help make decisions that will shape the programs, planning, organisation and instruction we devise for the children in our care.

Why evaluate anyway?

Evaluation should be a constant process, ever with us as we make our way through the day-to-day routines of the classroom. Yet though some of us see evaluation as fruitful, others see it merely as an unavoidable duty, while still others try to forget about it, hoping that when reporting time comes round they will somehow have accumulated enough information to permit accurate reporting. In many classrooms evaluation is the poor relation of the learning process. It is the part of planning a program or of classroom procedures that is added on at the end — an appendix that some would prefer forgotten as it seems bothersome, time-consuming and of no real value.

However, we must evaluate for a number of reasons. First, we must keep records of the progress of the children in our care because, as teachers, we are accountable. But accountable to whom? To the principal? To the parents? To our employers? To the children? I believe that to be accountable only to an external body, such as our employer, is not sufficient, though unfortunately some teachers feel powerless to move away from this concept of accountability. No — I believe, as Peter Johnston (1992) has demonstrated, that we must be *responsible* rather than accountable, because by being responsible we can become re-flective — about our teaching, our own learning and the children's learning.

Of course, if we do not show we are responsible, others will ensure that we are held accountable. Some outside body will endeavour to hold sway over classroom practices, and over that development of the skills, knowledge and attitudes of individuals which makes teaching one of the most important professions in the world. Do you really want that? Do you want politically oriented, external bodies telling you how your classroom should be run and what is best for children they have never seen? It is certainly not what I want. And if this is not what we want as a profession, then it is time we all became responsible — to the children we teach, to their parents, to the system we work for and, above all, to ourselves.

But how do we become more responsible? How do we make evaluation work for us rather than against us? How do we ensure that it is part of the social context of the classroom? I hope this book will help you to think about such issues before you make decisions about how to become responsible instead of simply being held accountable. It describes an evaluation program that involves not only the teacher but the children and their parents too. It will show you how to create within the class-room a social context which ensures that evaluation is part of the continuum of day-to-day events, and that the time you spend on it is not wasted collecting information that is never used.

Each of you is an individual, unique in your understanding and needs. The road you take towards implementing negotiated evaluation will be your own. But first let me tell you how I came to be a traveller on this road, so that you may better understand what is to follow.

Things no-one ever told me

All through my school years and beyond, I was scarcely ever told that I was good at anything. It was impressed on me that I had problems — reading problems, spelling problems, speech problems — but never that I was good at anything. The first inkling I had that I was not a complete failure was on the day I was informed that since there weren't enough copies of the maths test for the class and I was good at maths, I needn't do the test. You can imagine my thoughts. 'Me! Good at maths? Me who can't read? Me who can't spell? Me! Good at maths? Well, what do you know?'

Throughout my schooling I had this horrible feeling that I was always failing. I neither knew why, nor what was expected of me. I sat through interminable assemblies, always hoping that I would get an award but never being given one. I was frequently ridiculed in front of the class for my inefficiencies and my failure to comply with the norm.

When I became a teacher, I was determined to ensure that no child in my class should ever suffer in the same way as I felt I had done, and I was very diligent about it during my twenty years of classroom teaching. The opportunity to have an impact on classrooms other than my own came when I completed an MEd (Hons) thesis on literacy evaluation and decided to do some follow-up work on my findings, which ultimately led to the writing of this book.

You may be wondering by now how someone who could not 'read' or 'spell' was ever able to write a book. Well, about six years ago, I *was* told I could do something: I was told by someone whose opinion I valued that I could write. With that revelation I began to believe in myself as a writer and I began to write. Some children you teach may not get an opportunity such as this — the opportunity to believe in themselves and what they can do — unless you give it to them. The model of evaluation described in this book emphasises that positive communication with all children in your care is essential.

Underlying beliefs

A belief that *children* need to be involved in the evaluation process was the driving force behind the development of negotiated evaluation. My experience shows me that children are very capable of evaluating themselves, but, over and above that, I believe they have a right to know what is expected of them and that we, as teachers, need to know what they are thinking and what they expect of us. I believe teachers need to *negotiate* with children about what they know and understand and need to learn.

The other important 'players' in the process of negotiated evaluation are *parents*. The teacher needs to negotiate with parents about their understandings of their children's progress and about what progress and learning they see as important. Parents have much valuable knowledge about the development of their children, though many either feel they cannot adequately express it or do not realise that teachers value and need access to it. But we need to tap into this knowledge if we are to establish a meaningful and valid picture of each child. Both child and parents have the right to share what they know about the child's development, and negotiated evaluation helps them to exercise this right.

When we evaluate the children in our class, therefore, we must be prepared to negotiate with each of the players (the child and his or her parents) about what they already know and understand and about what they need to know and understand about learning and the child's progress. Ideally this negotiation should extend beyond the school and enhance the interaction between the child and parents at home. For this reason the major principle of negotiated evaluation is that there must be continual interaction between all those concerned with each child's learning, so that a full picture of the child's progress can be formed and acted upon.

Some may argue that administrators and politicians are players too, but as they basically require information only about the school population at large, rather than about individuals, they must take their place as observers. What is crucial is that information about each child's progress is able to travel freely between the players, so that valid judgements of merit and worth and better informed decisions about the future can be made.

CHAPTER ONE

The Origins of
Negotiated Evaluation

Current approaches to literacy evaluation

Currently literacy evaluation in Australia presents itself in varied forms. In at least one state, schools and teachers have the freedom to design their own systems provided that they participate in an annual state-wide testing program. Some state government bodies (for example, the Victorian Ministry of Education), with the very able assistance of consultants and practising teachers, have devised indicators (profiles) to guide teachers in making decisions about evaluation in the classroom and the school. However, adoption of these indicators requires a shift in the thinking, belief systems and evaluation practices of classroom teachers, away from a dependence on tests, marks and grades to a reliance on a rich description of what each child can do in an authentic classroom situation.

Some teachers have already made this shift. They have taken on board a variety of descriptive evaluation procedures, developed and trialled by literacy educators and classroom teachers to promote a better understanding and more valid use of profile indicators. However, as Wendy Crebbin (1992) has pointed out, different teaching approaches will constantly affect the use of such evaluation tools. The very open nature of profile descriptors leaves them subject to teacher interpretation, and therefore to misinterpretation.

Some commonly used procedures

In my experience, teachers rely less today than ten years ago on commercially designed tests of reading or spelling. They tend to use instead a variety of less formal, descriptive measures. In the area of reading, some of the most widely accepted descriptive procedures are running records, miscue analysis, cloze analysis and retelling. In order to exemplify the current status of literacy evaluation, particularly reading, I will describe each of them briefly.

Running records

Keeping running records is a very popular classroom procedure, first devised and described by Marie Clay (1979). There are probably two reasons for its popularity in Australia: firstly, it featured prominently in the ELIC (Early Literacy Inservice Course) program undertaken by thousands of teachers in the 1980s, and secondly (and more recently), it has become familiar to teachers in schools using Clay's reading recovery program.

The procedure requires the teacher to listen critically to the child's oral reading and to note any deviations from the original text. Particular attention is given to words omitted or substituted and to self-corrections attempted. These deviations from the text are noted on a score sheet and calculations are quickly made of the child's accuracy and self-correction rates. Special note is taken of the strategies the child is using to preserve the meaning of the text.

Miscue analysis

Miscue analysis originated in research by Kenneth Goodman (1982) into the nature of the reading process, but was soon adapted for use as a classroom evaluation tool. There are many different versions, some yielding more useful information than others. Miscue analysis is similar to the keeping of running records in that it involves the child in reading a text to the teacher while the teacher notes any deviations or miscues. The most obvious difference lies in the depth of the analysis. In miscue analysis attention is paid not only to self-correction and meaning-making strategies, but also to the reader's pattern of use of the syntactic, semantic and graphophonic cueing systems. Another difference is that the reader is required to orally retell the text just read aloud, allowing the teacher to gather another layer of information to support or modify the interpretation of the child's reading strategies gained from the analysis of miscues.

Cloze analysis

Cloze analysis, whereby deletions are made in a text and the reader is required to substitute a word for each deletion, is a means of evaluating silent reading strategies. A cloze passage constructed for evaluation purposes is one in which the deletions have been carefully selected to examine the reader's use of specific processing strategies, such as forward and backward referencing, or use of linguistic knowledge, real world knowledge and knowledge of the story line (Unsworth 1985). The reader's substitutions are analysed initially in terms of whether or not they preserve the passage's meaning, and then in terms of the strategies used to arrive at them. A post-cloze discussion will often provide more information about how the reader is processing text.

Retelling

Retelling is a classroom procedure of particularly wide appeal as it can be carried out either orally or as a written activity. It has most recently been popularised by the work of Brown and Cambourne (1987). The main emphasis is again on making meaning, using a text first read by the child and subsequently retold. Analysis concentrates on the construction of meaning, including (for a story) understanding the gist of the plot and the sequencing of events, and being aware of major characters and their traits and role within the story. Like cloze, written retelling can be carried out on a whole class basis, but the teacher needs to support any analysis of a written retelling by a follow-up discussion with the individual child.

Some cautions

Data collected from all these procedures should assist teachers not only in noting each child's progress, but also in aligning that progress with the appropriate indicators on a published profile. Care must be taken, however, not to fall into the trap of applying a deficit model of learning, whereby the child is seen as a failure should his or her behaviour not match the expected indicator. The emphasis should rather fall on what the child *can* currently do and what the next step in his or her development might be. Such an approach is exemplified in the developmental continua for reading and writing included in the WA Ministry of Education's *First Steps* program.

While the data from these procedures is very specific and quite helpful, the procedures themselves can be time-consuming and have been criticised by some as being of doubtful validity. For example, it has been argued (Bouffler 1992) that because their interpretation relies so much on the teacher's knowledge of the reading process, they may be used inappropriately by teachers who bring insufficient knowledge of literacy to them. Their validity is also in doubt if they are used only as 'one-off' tasks (this criticism, of course, is generally applied to the use of standardised tests).

Oral reading procedures, such as running records or miscue analysis, have come in for criticism on other counts. Concern has been expressed that oral reading is used to provide a window on the silent reading process, when in fact the two cannot properly be equated. The oral reading of a text tends to force the reader into a process of matching one word of written text to a spoken word, which may work against the selective sampling of print that is normal for effective readers. Another problem of miscue analysis (but not of running records) lies in the fact that the procedure only works if the reader makes sufficient errors ('miscues') for an analysis to be undertaken. For this reason, the text chosen by the teacher must be one which forces errors — that is, one at the reader's frustration level. We do not really know whether this contrived situation is provoking the reader into using strategies that he or she would not use if reading a text at his or her independent level of competence. The reader's lack of familiarity with the text may also affect the validity of miscue analysis as a measure of 'normal' classroom reading. Recently it has been suggested that the reader should be given the opportunity to preview the text before reading it aloud (Weaver 1990), so that miscue analysis can be closer to an authentic classroom oral reading situation.

Finally, the texts chosen for any of these procedures can vary greatly in context and form and so require of readers different kinds of semantic knowledge. Thus it is possible that what is being evaluated is the reader's prior knowledge of a field rather than his or her use of processing strategies. However, if teachers keep such concerns in mind when making use of these procedures, useful information can be obtained. The main strength of running records, miscue analysis, cloze analysis and retelling lies in their ability to provide the teacher with a detailed analysis of a child's reading behaviour.

A research project

In making instructional decisions, teachers use informal observation much more than any other form of evaluation. For some time, therefore, it has seemed to me that there is an important problem to be solved in ensuring that teachers' observations are as accurate, insightful and valid as possible, and it was partly with this in mind that, in 1987, I undertook a research project in a primary school in south-west Sydney. I wanted to know what evaluation procedures were being used and what happened to the data collected.

One of the first things I found was that evaluation data collected in classrooms was primarily used for reporting to parents and filling in records required by the employer. Accounting to these stakeholders (parents and the employer) seemed to be the most important consideration, for there was little evidence that teachers (or parents) were able to use the data to inform teaching or learning processes. I was driven to ask myself whether the teachers were being responsible or merely being held accountable.

Some other issues of concern to classroom teachers were highlighted by my research and deserve to be discussed here: the perceived purposes of evaluation, the use of checklists and anecdotal records, reporting to parents, and the use of time.

The purposes of evaluation

The teachers in the school under investigation *were* aware of the purposes of evaluation. They recognised that evaluation should be continuous and should result in changes to the teaching and learning program in order to accommodate children's individual needs. But, as I have indicated, this belief did not carry over into classroom practice. There was no evidence that it induced any change in their written programs or their teaching.

Checklists

Checklists presented real problems to the teachers I was studying. The ones they had developed in the school only allowed for the recording of the presence or absence of a particular literacy 'skill' — there was no mechanism whereby they could record any real progress or refinement in literacy behaviours. I have found this to be the case with most checklists that I have encountered; at best they can indicate the number of times a particular behaviour is sighted or some goal is achieved. In an effort to overcome this problem, teachers have devised a number of ingenious ways to indicate progress on a checklist. They may, for example, use a dot to indicate some progress, then a diagonal line to show further achievement, and finally a complete cross when full attainment of a specific skill has been noted. But even this is a crude measure of the real development that has occurred. It should be remembered that checklists are just that — lists to check that 'things' have been done. There is no way in which they can adequately reveal individual progress.

Many teachers find that the most valuable aspect of a checklist is the process of listing the behaviours to be observed. While it should not be expected that every teacher will create a set of criteria from scratch, just sifting through the numerous checklist items available from both commercial and personal sources can act as a stimulus for future observation, as it requires you to select, develop and formalise your ideas about what are important literacy behaviours, processes and products. After that, my experience is that checklists are best used as memory joggers when you are beginning your observations.

Anecdotal records

My research showed that the writing of descriptive notes about children was the most popular form of recording events in the classroom, but that the practice presented many problems. Although copious notes were taken, very little action ensued. Teachers continued with programs already in place irrespective of what their notes told them (with the possible exception of incidental changes made intuitively as they carried out their day-to-day routines). It appeared that they did not stop to look at the discoveries they had made. In other words, they collected data but did not analyse it.

In addition, many teachers felt it was a waste of time adding anecdotal records to a child's personal profile, since they believed that next year's teacher would not be interested in them for a number of reasons. Someone else's notes can be very difficult to read, and they are after all someone else's: most teachers wanted the opportunity to form their own 'unbiased' opinion of each child.

As a teacher I have found further problems with anecdotal records when used on a whole class basis. Because in any class there are some children who continually gain the teacher's attention, more notes are taken about the behaviour of these children, and their progress or lack of it. Unfortunately most of these notes are negative in tone, since it is usually the children experiencing difficulty who attract most attention. They have what I call a negative 'halo'. At the other end of the spectrum you find the children about whom you would like to say 'I taught them everything they know', although you are aware that they will learn under most circumstances — sometimes despite you. These children also gain attention and their behaviours, usually praiseworthy, are observed and noted. They have a positive 'halo'.

But what of the other children in the class: the middle-of-the-road children, the 'quiet achievers' and the 'plodders'? My research revealed that in many cases there were few notes, if any, on these children. Even when an effort was made to record their progress, the comments were usually very general: for example, 'is progressing satisfactorily'. Yet every child deserves the teacher's attention — every child should be considered, not only those who are most noteworthy. In practice, however, it would seem that to make this truism a reality is a very difficult task indeed.

Reporting to parents

The age-old issue of reporting to parents always comes up whenever the subject of evaluation is discussed. What part does the biannual report play in the process of evaluation? The teachers in my study viewed it mainly as an accountability exercise, done largely because it was seen as part of the structure of schooling. This accords with my broader experience: generally reporting is carried out in a variety of ways, all of them time-consuming but few of them productive in terms of their influence on what actually goes on in the classroom. Again, reporting is something we just 'have to do'.

Many reporting systems involve checking boxes that characterise the child as performing 'sometimes', 'usually' or 'never', or use some similar compilation of descriptors that are applied on the basis of predetermined criteria. In most forms of reporting, I believe, the categories of behaviour selected for report are arbitrary, and the order in which the descriptors are arranged and the space allocated for each are in direct proportion to the importance placed on each discipline by the school or system. Some reporting systems provide space for descriptive comment too, but this is usually limited to two to three lines. How can six months' progress be adequately described in three lines?

Many schools appear to be in an almost constant state of flux with their reporting systems because they are dissatisfied with them. They are either in the process of changing the report form or have just changed it and are in the first stages of implementation. It seems to me that a tremendous amount of time is being spent with few positive results.

The teachers with whom I worked in my research admitted that the report forms they used were very bland and not of much consequence. Most felt they had enough information in their heads to be able to write their class reports without consulting the other data they had so conscientiously collected. So why were they spending so much time on evaluation?

The other concern I have about current reporting practices is the way in which parents often misinterpret the information provided on the report. When grades are given, some parents will tend to accord these greater credence than any written comment. For others, it does not matter what the 'A' or 'C' is for: they will insist upon counting and comparing grades, and thereby misinterpret completely what teachers have spent hours organising and writing. This not only indicates that changes are required in current reporting procedures, but also that parents need to be given a more realistic understanding of what schooling is about.

Problems with time

Time was seen as an overwhelming constraint by the teachers I worked with in my research project. They couldn't possibly find any more time for evaluation — there were no more hours in the day! One of the main reasons they felt this way was that they saw themselves as the *only* evaluators of the children in their care. In addition, they were generally setting tasks and tests to evaluate progress as 'add-on' activities, and they were not using other sources of evaluation, such as the children themselves.

Their management of time in the classroom also needed reconsideration. I believe that if you do not manage your classroom time efficiently, your evaluation procedures will not be productive. One way of determining how productive is the time spent on evaluation is to ask yourself whether it is 'negative' or 'positive' time. If you are spending a lot of time collecting data but not doing anything with it, then you are in negative time — you are wasting time. If, on the other hand, you are collecting and analysing data from a variety of sources and perspectives and making judgements of merit and worth about it, and if this process is helping you to make decisions about future planning and is informing learning, then you are in 'positive' time. The teachers I was studying wanted to tip the balance from negative to positive but didn't know how to set about it.

What I assume

In this chapter I have proclaimed some of the beliefs I have evolved in over twenty years of teaching and working with teachers. There are also some assumptions I make about evaluation that should be spelled out here to allow you, the reader, and me, the writer, to gain common ground.

All evaluation procedures and tools you use should be in accord with your theory of teaching and learning.

Every evaluation activity should have as its basis the same theory as the teaching and learning practices it is designed to evaluate. It is awkward, to say the least, to teach with one theory as a framework for what one is doing, and then to try to evaluate effectively with approaches based on a different theory. For example, if you believe that reading is a process of bringing meaning to and extracting meaning from print, then it is pointless to test sight recognition of a list of isolated and arbitrarily chosen words, devoid of context and therefore devoid of other cues to meaning. Nevertheless many teachers, I find, go on trying to reconcile contradictory teaching and evaluative practices, and the continued use of some evaluation tools which originated up to fifty years ago serves to encourage this anomaly.

Evaluation practices set up outside the normal learning environment are less valid than those which occur as part of normal learning.

If an evaluation procedure requires changes in the physical, emotional or pedagogical environment of learning, the accuracy of the evaluation will be diminished. If children are used to working in groups with their desks clustered together and then all of a sudden, due to 'test conditions', they have to cover their work so that no-one else can see it, the results of that test situation cannot be seen as a valid reflection of their learning behaviours. If a teacher chooses to hear a child read aloud as a measure of reading competence when the normal practice in the class is for children to read silently, any evaluation of that reading will be invalid. If children are placed in a stressful situation or in unfamiliar surroundings for the purposes of evaluation, the results will be suspect. To determine just how valid are some of the evaluative situations foisted upon them, teachers need to become aware of the possible incongruities. If procedures do require a break from normal classroom routines, we must allow children time to familiarise themselves with the differences.

No evaluation strategy or source is valid on its own.

Evaluation decisions based on only one source of information are dangerous. Two or more informative strategies or information sources are necessary to give additional perspectives and validate conclusions. Not only do you need to collect data from a variety of sources, but over a period of time too: decisions should not be based on one evaluative occasion. For example, listening to a child read once will not tell you accurately how he or she is progressing in reading and what strategies are being used. Evaluation cannot be done 'on the hop' or thought about at the last minute. It has to be thoroughly planned and incorporated in the day-to-day procedures of the classroom.

Children and their abilities have an intrinsic value and individual worth which cannot be adequately described by a ranking, number or letter grade.

School administrations often require results to be reduced to a letter for reporting to parents, or to a number for school or system record cards. An argument continually advanced in support of this practice is that parents want marks for their children, so that they know where they are coming in the class. However, I do not believe it is for the benefit of their children that parents request this information — it is really so that they can compare their child with others. But, as Eisner (1979) pointed out: 'If we want to know if a child has grown taller, it is fruitless to find out if he/she is above average height.' It seems to me that if parents are well informed about their child's development, in terms they can understand, they will be less inclined to want to make such comparisons.

Conclusion

When I had considered all the issues and assumptions outlined in this chapter, it became obvious that there was much more work to be done on evaluation if any progress was to be made, and if teachers were to stave off the threat of being simply *held accountable* rather than being recognised as actively *taking responsibility* for what happens in their classrooms. What follows in this book is an account of the work I have done in many schools to try to solve some of the problems.

CHAPTER TWO

The Development of a Model

Prior to the development of negotiated evaluation, interaction between parents, teachers and children in the evaluation process was often very limited. As a teacher I would send reports home to parents, sometimes in a sealed envelope, and seldom with the child having any prior knowledge of the report's contents. I would receive a minimal response to these reports, usually in the form of 'courtesy' comments by several parents, who would thank me for a good year with their child or remark that they were pleased with the progress indicated. I always hoped for more input during subsequent parent-teacher interviews, but it was rarely forthcoming, probably because the parents saw themselves as being relatively powerless in such a situation. They expected me to ask the questions and they would respond, but there was very little interchange of valuable ideas and information. I am sure that many of you have experienced similar frustrations.

When I found that my own experiences were echoed by those of the teachers in my case study, I began to think more carefully about the notion that parents were another source of information for evaluation, as yet untapped. After all, they were in a position to provide a unique perspective on their children's progress and development.

The teachers in my case study indicated that their interaction with children over evaluation was similarly limited — in the main they carried out the procedures and recorded the results without consulting the children individually. However, I do not believe we can hope to evaluate the children in our care comprehensively if we don't ask them what they are thinking, what they understand and what they know. Likewise, what we have found out about children and their learning, and the goals we have for them, should be shared with them. In the past there have been many things kept secret from children in the classroom (for example, what the teacher's expectations were, or what had been observed about a child's developmental progress), and little or no credence has been given to the children's own ideas about their progress. On this count too, then, evaluation and any planning that has flowed from it have been markedly one-sided.

With all this in mind, I searched the highways and byways until I was able to put together a plan that seemed as if it might begin to answer the twin problems of better involving parents and children in the evaluation process and making better use of the time spent and the data collected. A number of my friends played important parts in this search.

Two colleagues

Sue Dockett, a colleague at the University of Western Sydney, Macarthur, helped me to formulate the idea that classroom observations need to be planned. This led to the idea of organising anecdotal record keeping so as to accommodate every child in the class and avoid the 'halo' effects mentioned in the previous chapter. With Sue's help, I conceived the notion of *focused observation*, whereby the teacher focuses her attention (for evaluation purposes) on five or six children for a week at a time, rotating through the class. This means that she is continuously collecting and analysing data but ensures that each child gains a fair share of her attention. Subsequently I matched the notion of focused observation with one of *continuous reporting to parents*. Instead of saving up data for a mid-year or end-of-year report, why not report to parents as soon as observations have been made and data has been analysed?

Another colleague who played an important role in the development of negotiated evaluation was Alison Preece. In 1988 I had the pleasure of meeting Alison when she was visiting Australia from the University of Victoria in British Columbia. At the time I was looking carefully at the part parents might play in the evaluation process, and a project that Alison was involved in gave rise to many ideas. She had been working with some teachers on the development of observation sheets for parents to use with their children (Anthony et al. 1991). It seemed to me that sheets like these would help fill the gap in communications between classroom teacher and parents, and so I offered to field-test them in Australia.

The model in embryo

It was in this way that the idea of negotiated evaluation began to evolve. There were three aspects essential to its structure:

1   continual interaction between the players

2   collection of data from a variety of sources and perspectives

3   analysis of this data and the writing of reports to inform each of the players.

The continual interaction consisted of:

- focused observation by the teacher followed by discussions between teacher and child

- input from the child through discussion and self-evaluation

- interaction between teacher and parents by way of parent observation or profile sheets.

The collection of data comprised:

- observations by parents, teacher and child over time and in a variety of situations

- samples of work products selected by both child and teacher.

The analysis of the data was achieved through:

- making decisions about the merit and worth of both the processes (behaviours) and products observed

- collating these decisions to write a number of reports spread through the year.

The interaction involved in negotiated evaluation is best represented in a simple diagram:

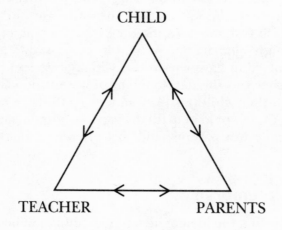

Figure 2.1

One thing I didn't properly consider when first constructing this model was the third side of the triangle — the interaction between child and parents. However, once I began to pilot my approach, first at Nareena Hills Public School and then at Thomas Acres Public School (both in NSW), my oversight was quickly remedied. Two things happened. At Nareena Hills, parents were asked to complete a mid-year report on what they and their child considered had been the main indicators of progress through the previous six months. At Thomas Acres, teachers started to request written responses from parents on each child's reports. They allocated not simply a line or two at the bottom of the report, but a section on the back equal to at least half the space occupied by the report itself. Space was similarly allocated for the child to respond to what both teacher and parents had written. And so a stronger interaction between parents and child began to emerge.

Two types of information

There is one other important consideration I need to mention at this point, and that is the place of quantitative and qualitative information

With negotiated evaluation reports no longer travel in sealed envelopes; instead they are discussed between teacher and child before being taken home.

within the model. Quantitative information, generally speaking, is data that involves some process of measurement or ranking, and it is usually represented by numbers, percentages or grades. Qualitative information, on the other hand, seeks to describe something rather than measure the amount of it. In primary education it involves the description of children's behaviours and achievements, and so it's particularly well suited to charting individual progress and describing the quality of learning processes and products.

While some educators believe there is a place for both types of evaluation, my own view is that quantitative evaluation has very limited uses in the primary classroom, especially as literacy is not a single, monolithic entity which can be represented numerically. Many critics of qualitative evaluation argue that the description involved is too subjective and too susceptible to teacher bias. But all evaluation procedures and materials, including observation and the use of tests (whether standardised or not), are subjective to some degree. Evaluators, including test designers, bring to the task their own biases, including a set of beliefs as to what constitutes valuable knowledge. However, teachers can become aware of their own biases and try to take them into account when observing children's behaviour. It is not subjectivity that causes problems so much as a lack of knowledge and understanding about the nature of relevant data and insufficient sources of collection.

Negotiated evaluation, then, involves primarily the collection, interpretation and reporting of qualitative information. It focuses on the individual quality of each child's learning processes and products, in order that all those involved in the child's progress can get to know the child better and become better able to assist him or her in the learning processes required for future development.

Looking ahead

In the remaining chapters of this book you will find a number of procedures recommended as part of the process of negotiated evaluation. Some are not new, while others have been developed by myself and my colleagues over the past few years. All of them, however, involve interaction between at least two participants in the evaluation process — that is, between child and teacher, child and parent, or teacher and parent.

The difficulty with such an interactive model is to separate the information into discrete sets, as there is naturally a good deal of overlap. To impose some order on my material, I have chosen one of the participants as the focus of each of the next three chapters (in turn, the teacher, the parent and the child), and I have allocated various procedures to these chapters on the basis of who the main participant is in any particular procedure. So, for example, I discuss focused observation in the next chapter because that is devoted to 'The Teacher's Role'.

CHAPTER THREE

The Teacher's Role

Although the teacher is not necessarily the major player in negotiated evaluation, the teacher's role is pivotal to the process and so is best discussed first. It includes not only data collection and analysis, but also initiating, encouraging and negotiating the involvement of the other players (parents and children) — an aspect covered in Chapters 4 and 5. The procedures and classroom organisation recommended for data collection are discussed in this chapter, while the analysis of the data and its various uses are discussed in Chapter 6.

Focused observation

Observation is one of the key procedures in any classroom evaluation program, and in negotiated evaluation it is particularly important for all the participants to be keen and perceptive observers. However, my research on anecdotal records had made clear the need for a more systematic way of organising children and classrooms so as to ensure that every child's behaviours were adequately observed and recorded — not merely those of the attention-seekers or the children whose performance was in some way outstanding. Thus, as mentioned in the previous chapter, I began to develop the notion of focused observation.

The focusing means that instead of trying to observe as many children in the class as possible at any one time, the teacher selects about five or six children to concentrate on over, say, one or two weeks. That small group of children is observed closely and anecdotal records are made. (Most children love being observed and are not bothered by being the focus of attention.) Then concentration shifts to another group of five or six, and so on. Thus every child is the focus of careful observation for four to six periods a year, in addition to the ongoing incidental observation normal in any classroom.

Probably children will be randomly selected for observation, and so will range in ability and needs, but selection can be on the basis of a previously established class grouping. For example, Sue, a teacher who took part in the pilot study of negotiated evaluation at Nareena Hills Public School, used her maths groups to select her focus children. One reason was that these groups were timetabled to operate first thing Monday morning, and so the focused observation began right at the start of the week. It was also a time when Sue had parent helpers in the room, which made it easier to devote time to the focus group without feeling that the remainder of the class were being neglected. Each group successively was the focus of Sue's observation for five days, during which she was able to watch them closely in a variety of situations across the whole curriculum.

Thomas, the 'middle-of-the-class', quiet achiever

'Yes, it's those middle-of-the-class children that really miss out,' one teacher, Chris, reported to me after using focused observation for a short time. One boy in her class, Thomas, was a quiet achiever. He sat and achieved what she expected. His reading and writing were average, but his speaking capabilities seemed only fair. After focusing on Thomas for the nominated five days, Chris discovered that his mother was a keen whale watcher and was involved in many whale-watching expeditions in boats. What Thomas didn't know about whales wasn't worth knowing! Chris decided to encourage him to make use of this knowledge and lead a group within the class to research whales. This seemed to be just what was wanted to help Thomas bloom. Chris no longer regards him as 'just average' — he is excelling, in part because she took the time to talk to a child who might otherwise have missed out because his performance did not make him particularly visible to the teacher.

Recording observations

Observation in itself is not sufficient — to be useful, observations must be faithfully recorded. An important factor here is that the closer to the time of observation the recording is done, the more accurate it will be.

Every teacher who has embarked on negotiated evaluation has discovered a different way of recording his or her observations. I will describe a few of these ways, but no doubt every fresh recruit will discover yet another way to do it, either by modifying the suggestions given here or by combining them with other ideas currently in use.

Single sheets

Each child is allocated a single observation sheet, which can be headed with the child's name, the date and/or the week and term. Added to these can be any key points you want to pick up on in your observation, or key areas you want to note. Initially Sue used such a sheet, with the headings 'Language/English', 'Maths' and 'Social Behaviour'. That seemed to work, but as time went by other curriculum areas had to be added, and eventually the sheet included 'Attitude' in an endeavour to cover cross-curricular learning behaviours. The intention is to add other such learning characteristics in the near future.

Sue carried the relevant sheets with her as she moved around the room and entered notes as she made her observations. The first time she tried focused observation her records were fairly scant, probably because the whole concept was new to her. She also found that often she did not have her sheets handy at the moment of observation, but this was

Observation needn't be silent. Often the best notes are written after talking to children about what they are doing.

rectified by attaching them with a pen to a clipboard. The clipboard also held a class list, so that any noteworthy experiences of children not the current focus of observation could be recorded.

One for all

Some teachers trialling negotiated evaluation found it cumbersome to use a different sheet for each child. They preferred to have one sheet divided into sections in which they could record their observations of all five children. Because of the quantity of information to be recorded, two or three of these sheets were sometimes required for each week's observations.

Observation grid

I have seen two forms of grid used. One is a single sheet of paper (A3), divided into six sections vertically, with one section for each key learning area, and into five or six sections horizontally, one for each child to be observed (Figure 3.1). This sheet is left ready on the teacher's desk and observations are added to it either at the time of observation or shortly afterwards.

	English	Maths	Science & Tech	Human Soc...	Creative Arts	PE Health
Joanna						
Miriam						
Mitchell						
Louise						
Jicinta						
Lupcho						

Figure 3.1 *Observation grid*

26/3
Reading: flicking pages, left
   to right, top to bottom
Writing: settled, reread
   piece, added, edited

                              BB

Observations of beginning
reader and writer

24/5
Maths: organising small
   group to measure
   classroom objects;
   concepts 'longer than',
   'shorter than' used

                              DR

Observations of beginning
mathematician

15/6
Maths: defined problem,
   decided on and
   implemented plan of
   action, reflected on
   process

                              JK

Observations of proficient
problem solver

4/8
Reading: understands
   character relationships
   and their changing roles
   (character web)
Writing: assisted peer in
   editing report, explaining
   use of paragraphing

                              4J

Observations of proficient
reader and writer

Figure 3.2

The other type of grid is one where only the children's names appear
on the grid and the observations are recorded on 'post-it' pad squares
carried around by the teacher. These are then placed under the child's
name on the grid at an appropriate time. The advantage here is that the
post-it pads are small, convenient to carry and hence less likely to be
forgotten or to interfere with normal teaching behaviours. But if you try

this method, don't forget to put the child's initials in the corner of each note to prevent any mix-up (Figure 3.2).

On the desk

Instead of placing the post-it notes on a grid, the teacher can place them on the child's desk, which involves the child more in the process. (However, it's still advisable to write the child's initials in the corner of each note.) Some teachers place a sheet of paper on the desk of each child being observed. This not only allows the teacher to record observations swiftly, but can also be used to encourage the child to add his or her comments or to question the teacher's comments, so that they become more meaningful. At the end of the observation period the post-it notes or sheets are allocated to children's individual files for categorisation and report writing.

Audio tape

One school staff thought they might try to tape their observations on voice-activated tape recorders, which are portable, battery-operated and small enough to be kept in your pocket. However, they found that while they were indeed able to capture observations immediately, there were some inherent problems, such as background noise levels and the time-consuming task of transcribing the tapes.

Conventional cassette recorders are still a convenient way of tracking young children's progress in oral reading, provided that there is a tape for each child and each fresh recording is dated. The teacher, child and parent can review the tape periodically and note growth in fluency and confidence.

Robyn Hutchins, a teacher from St Bernadette's Primary School, Castle Hill, NSW, has told me of another way in which she uses audio tapes. She records teacher-child discussions. Not only is the tape a permanent record of the discussion, but it is sent home to parents so that they can listen to the interaction and learn more about what happens in Robyn's classroom and how their child responds to different ideas. A brilliant idea, thank you, Robyn.

Video tape

Some of the teachers I have been working with have found videotaping of great value when they are observing. Some have been able to set up the video camera in their rooms and leave it running, while others have asked a 'buddy' teacher to act as camera operator. If you try the latter, you will find that sitting down with your buddy afterwards and discussing the results will greatly enhance your observation skills. But however you manage it, remember that the camera should be focused on the children, not on you!

Summary

I must admit that my favourite recording method is the 'On the desk' one. Nevertheless this can be problematic in the lower grades when children are far less 'attached' to their desks, or in other grades if your classroom organisation discourages children from having their own desks. Perhaps some form of card that children keep with them could be the answer.

Other evaluative procedures

Product collection

In negotiated evaluation, the teacher's role is to observe not only the learning processes and behaviours of the children being focused on, but also to take a close look at the products of their work. The period of focused evaluation is an ideal time to collect work samples from each

An exchange about a particular piece of work can sometimes lead to a more general exploration of a child's attitudes.

group. Samples should always be dated, and it's a good idea to write a couple of comments on the bottom or back, highlighting the progress that's been made. Even if a product is difficult to retain as a sample (for example, a mobile, diorama or something designed in a science and technology unit), some anecdotal record of it can be jotted down.

Exploring attitudes

In addition, observations should be made of children's understandings and attitudes. This can only be done by consulting with each child about how he or she feels about various areas of schooling. Sometimes this may take the form of an interview, or the child may be asked to complete a self-evaluation sheet (see Chapter 5). Wherever possible, the child should

---

Never assume

Janni was nine years old and couldn't read. During reading time she exhibited classical avoidance behaviour. She had been tested; she had been in many remedial programs, but she still couldn't interact with a book. It might be assumed that there was some learning difficulty, and that if the school kept 'remediating' her, there could be a breakthrough. However, one day, when talking with Janni during focused observation time, her teacher asked whether anyone at home liked reading. 'Yes,' Janni scowled, 'Mum does.' It came out in the ensuing conversation that Janni's mother was an avid reader of popular romantic novels, to the point of having a book-holder on the bench in the kitchen so that she could read while preparing meals or washing up. Whenever Janni wanted to talk to her mum she was too busy reading. 'I hate reading,' she said. 'I'll never read if it means I can't talk to people.' Now the teacher had something to work on in beginning to solve Janni's problem.

---

be party to any observations made as a result of this consultation. Some possible starting points, tapping the children's learning and understanding, could be questions such as these, borrowed in part from the Burke interview (Goodman, Watson and Burke 1987):

- *What books do you like to read?*
- *Who reads/writes at home?*
- *Who is the best reader you know? Why?*
- *How would you help someone having trouble with reading/writing?*

- *How come you made the decision to . . . ?*

- *What do you do when . . . ?*

Often we believe that as teachers we know why children react to situations in the way they do, but sometimes our assumptions are proved wrong. Talking with the children we have chosen to focus on is one good way of clarifying our interpretations of classroom behaviour.

Management of time

Time seems to be the recurring preoccupation of teachers in this and all other types of classroom evaluation. Time has to be well spent, adding to your knowledge and the child's development. It must also be remembered that evaluation is not an 'add-on' — not something to be done as a result of learning, after a set of activities has been completed — it is part of the learning, part of the activities. It should be happening all the time, and as teachers we must become adept at the practice of evaluating continually during the day as children are working.

Classroom organisation

Have you been able to find sufficient time during the day to observe children? Clever classroom organisation can help you by allowing you more time to observe and record your observations. I can best illustrate what I mean by describing a class which I observed recently in a school in New Hampshire.

Pat McLure's Year 1/2 class had been together for only a month, but already many strategies and organisational features were well established. In most classrooms the responsibility for the class's operation lies with the teacher. Here it was firmly (though unobtrusively) in the hands of the children.

The children were, for example, responsible for marking the attendance register. Each child had a card in a pocket on a wall chart with his or her name on one side and name and photo on the other. On entering the room, or soon afterwards, they were each responsible for turning their cards over so that the photo side faced outwards. Later the child in charge of monitoring attendance would check those present against the class list. The children were responsible for reversing their cards before leaving at the end of the day.

The children were also responsible for organising the sharing sessions. Sharing was scheduled three times a day. Two children could share their work with the remainder of the class in the morning (writing), one after recess (reading) and one more in the afternoon (free choice). One child would be responsible for 'signing up' those who wished to share. During the course of the morning she or he would circulate around the room with a clipboard holding the sign-up sheet (Figure 3.3) and a class list. Those children who had not already shared during that week (according to the class list) were asked it they wanted to share. If they did, they were checked off the class list and signed up.

Day............................ Date..................

Sharing writing

Signed..

Sharing reading

Signed..

Sharing free choice

Signed..

Reading circle

Signed..

Signed..

Signed..

Signed..

Signed..

Figure 3.3 *Sign-up sheet*

Signing up for reading circle was organised in a similar manner, as were recess and lunch orders. The rostering of the classroom jobs for each week was undertaken by a child the previous week. Apart from these overall classroom responsibilities, the day was centred on the individual. If a child forgot to bring in his folder from home, the teacher discussed how he might remember the next day, and it was then his responsibility to remember. All children were aware of the daily program as they moved from one experience to another. Those who were not sure were assisted by other children in a manner which encouraged them to take responsibility for themselves in the future. This common assumption of responsibility was evident in the reading circle when a particular child, on coming to a word she did not know, tried several strategies, discussed the word with the other children, answered their questions and only relinquished ownership of the problem when she wanted to. All the time she was in control, taking responsibility.

During sharing time the children who had signed on had a set time limit (about ten minutes each), the aim being to generate discussion about their reading or writing. The set period encouraged concentrated discussion and ensured that each sharer had enough time. All the children took responsibility for monitoring the time limit, and someone gently reminded the sharer when it was nearly up.

The children took responsibility for choice of topic in writing, choice of book in reading and choice of activity in the afternoon when learning centres were used. All the while the teacher was working with small groups and individuals, evaluating their progress and promoting their development.

Because the children were comfortable but challenged, because they were organised but responsible, because they worked together but maintained ownership, the room was quiet but busy, individualised but interactive, teacher-guided but child-centred. The teacher extended her responsibility by taking extensive observation notes during sharing time and reading circle.

Altogether this classroom was a shining example of teacher and children taking responsibility. The result was an effective and stimulating learning environment, and it is worth exploring in more detail some of the processes and practices that had evolved, particularly the ones that can help in the organisation of other classrooms and allow more time for specific observations.

Sharing a piece of writing during sharing time

The signed-up child was in charge of the class. He read and discussed what he had written. He was responsible for the interaction and the time, although the other children monitored that as well. Meanwhile the teacher sat off to one side and took copious notes of the interaction. What a splendid opportunity to observe the five children under focus that week!

Sharing reading during sharing time

The signed-up child read aloud to the children from a book she had chosen and then asked questions to initiate discussion. This was a time involving considerable interaction. Another child might comment that he wanted to get that book in quiet time so that he could read the rest of the story. Again the teacher was able to observe and make notes.

Reading circle

Reading circle involved four or five signed-up children coming together to discuss or read from the book they were currently working on. Children had free choice of books and read for a variety of purposes, but it was expected that each child would share at some time during the week, either with a reading circle or with the whole class. During reading circles the teacher, although active in helping the children pursue the discussion, did not dominate it. Each child discussed or read his or her selected book while the teacher observed, interacting where necessary to promote learning and noting the needs of each child involved.

Using co-observers

Another method that you may find helpful when organising your classroom for observing is to develop a buddy or co-observer system with another teacher. This is ideal in a team or co-operative teaching situation but may be done in a variety of other situations. The basis of the method is to arrange for a buddy teacher either to assume responsibility for your class while you observe or to observe while you teach. This approach has been used extensively in many schools where I have worked, and teachers have found that it is sometimes easier to observe when they are not responsible for 'delivery'. They have reported gaining a far deeper understanding of the children they are observing and the processes they are experiencing, as well as further developing their observation skills.

What should the teacher look for while observing?

In order to establish what to look for while observing, you may need to give some thought to the purpose of particular activities. Ask yourself, 'Why have I set this activity? How will I know when the purpose has been achieved?' In other words, you need know what you are expecting children to learn. The examples below of what you might look for are drawn from literature-based teaching strategies widely used in primary classrooms, and I have discussed them in a way which I hope will assist you in expressing your purposes and expected outcomes.

However, before coming to these examples, I wish to draw your attention to the issue of *unexpected outcomes*. It is important not to be so controlled by your expected outcomes that you lose sight of the unexpected ones, as it is these that will alert you to the individual needs of each child. For example, an unexpected outcome of discussion after a reading of *Possum Magic* might be the need for children to investigate the geographical location of the cities mentioned, although the prime purpose of the lesson was for them to examine what might constitute typical Australian food.

Text patterns

One purpose of activities such as story maps, story ladders and retelling is to encourage children to demonstrate their understanding of the patterning of ideas in a variety of texts. As a child recalls and thinks through, say, a narrative in the process of reconstructing it as a story map, he or she will be drawing on an understanding of text patterns. The teacher should then be able to use the completed story map (and any observations of the child during its construction, or discussions afterwards) as evidence of the child's developing knowledge of the elements of narrative and how they are patterned.

Character relationships

The broad purpose of activities such as literary sociograms, readers theatre and role plays is for children to develop and demonstrate their understanding of the relationships between characters in a narrative. Teachers might look closely at a completed literary sociogram to see whether the reader has charted effectively the main character's relationships with other characters, what inferences have been drawn about the nature of these relationships and what other insights are evident. In role plays or readers theatre, understanding will be demonstrated through the verbal and physical expression used in recreating the character. Because children are developing a deeper understanding of the relationships between fictional characters, teachers can also observe and discuss with them the way relationships between characters are developed in their own written work.

Character development

The purpose of literary character interviews, literary report cards and character profiles is to show the quality of children's understanding of how characters develop and change over time within a narrative. In analysing completed work of this kind, teachers can examine children's ability to pull together information about characters from different parts of the text, as well as whether they have drawn inferences beyond ideas directly stated by the author. Children's ability to apply their concepts of character development can be gauged by looking to see whether they can develop interesting and believable characters in their own writing.

A challenge

When I first started working with negotiated evaluation, I could see that the ultimate challenge would be to avoid being bound by the key learning areas and instead find a means of observing behaviours across the whole curriculum — behaviours which are markers of the learning processes underlying all primary school learning and which are a truer indication of a child's progress than mastery of content. Problem solving and risk taking are examples of the kind of behaviours I mean. In an attempt to meet this challenge, I devised an observation sheet with headings for attitude, processes, participation and response. This was trialled in one school but soon abandoned, as the teachers found it too difficult to implement a new system (negotiated evaluation) and take on a different view of learning outcomes at the same time. As mentioned earlier in this chapter, Sue from Nareena Hills has started to use 'attitude' as a focus, but the idea has gone no further in Australia. In British Columbia, however, I saw a similar idea in action.

Joy Paquin, one of the teachers I have most enjoyed observing, was working with Alison Preece, Norma Mickleson, Terry Johnson and Robert Anthony. They had been considering the characteristics of good learning. Some they had isolated were risk taking, self-esteem, creativity, generativeness (the capacity for coming up with ideas and initiatives), humour, responsibility, knowledge, empathy and resourcefulness. Instead of listing these characteristics and then trying to look for them when observing children's behaviours, Joy first observed and recorded the behaviours and later attempted to categorise them. She would record her observations on small post-its and afterwards sit down with the child's observation folder to make decisions about the essential learning characteristics that each recorded behaviour represented. The observation folder had a grid drawn on the inside cover, with each of the characteristics she was concentrating on heading a square on the grid. As she categorised each observation she placed it in the corresponding square (Figure 3.4).

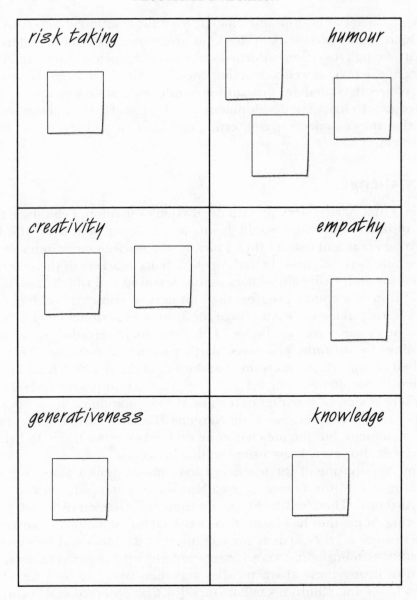

Figure 3.4 *Grid using characteristics of good learning*

So the idea was not to observe under headings but to categorise the observations after they were made. Was this where I went wrong originally? The challenge to you is to decide what you believe are the characteristics of good learning and try this procedure out for yourself. I'm sure it will not only inform you but will eventually become a pivotal point of your observation.

CHAPTER FOUR

Involving Parents

The important role that parents can play in the evaluation of a child's progress has traditionally been ignored by education systems. However, in negotiated evaluation that role is not only recognised but greatly valued — indeed, it is seen as vital to the success of the program. But in order to create the necessary links between parents and teachers, and to strengthen the links between parents and their children, a number of procedures need to be built into the framework of the classroom evaluation program. They include descriptive reports to which both parent and child are asked to respond, parent observation profiles, parent-written reports, communication books, evaluation books, portfolios and child-led conferences. (These last three items are discussed in Chapter 5, which focuses on the children's role.) Most of the practical examples in this chapter come from Nareena Hills Public School, as it was there that I piloted the idea of negotiated evaluation.

Communication between teachers and parents

Before parents can become more involved in the evaluation of their children, several processes have to be put in place. First of all you should notify the parents that there is going to be a change in the evaluation system. You might like to use as a model the letter reproduced overleaf. It was composed by staff at Nareena Hills, drawing on material developed for the use of schools in British Columbia (Anthony et al. 1991). Other school staffs have already adapted this letter to meet their own needs, and you'll find an example of one such adaptation in Chapter 7.

A meeting of parents is also a useful forum for explaining the changes envisaged. The main emphasis in the schools where such meetings have been held has been on the fact that we value what parents know about their children, and on the ways we will help them tell *us* what *they* know.

Dear Parent,

Your child has embarked on an exciting adventure this year. She is going to be learning all sorts of new things. While the responsibility for this learning rests with the child, you as parents and myself as teacher will need to be aware, alert and supportive of our young learner.

It is important that you and I co-operate to focus our attention on the progress your child is making. In order for me to report more consistently on each child's progress, I've decided to send a report to several families each week. I hope this will help you to know more about the progress your child is making. It will also include some suggestions as to how you can help her learning at home.

I'll also send you some guidelines so that you can send me reports on your child's learning at home. These guidelines will focus on the types of behaviours you could notice about her as she grows as a learner.

(Principal) is keen to be involved in this approach to evaluating progress too. We're sure that together, children, parents and teachers, we can help your child achieve her full potential.

Kind regards

_____   _____

(Principal)   (Teacher)

A letter from Nareena Hills: two were written (one for parents of girls, one for parents of boys) to avoid the impersonal tenor of he/she and his/her.

Parents' responses to descriptive reports

Most schools leave a space for parents at the end of their report form, but usually this only amounts to a line or two for comment, with another line for the parent's signature. What message does this give the parent? It definitely does not say, 'We think you know a lot about your child'! It definitely does not say, 'We value what you know about your child'! It really says, 'Comment if you can, but don't forget to sign the report so that we know you've seen it, because we can't trust your child to show it to you'.

I believe that the prominence and amount of space given on the report for parent response is directly related to the type and quality of that response. In negotiated evaluation, this issue is dealt with by providing a much longer section for parental comment. Another factor is the nature of the report. Since the reports written in negotiated evaluation are descriptive, rather than a listing of grades or numerical scores, parents have something much more meaningful to respond to.

Together with additional measures such as parent observation sheets, the invitation to parents to report back to the teacher has caused some amazing changes in parent response. Some schools now supply an additional sheet and invite both the parents and the child to respond on it. Other schools leave the whole of the reverse side of the report clear for responses. Whichever way it is done, the message to parents is clear: 'We believe you know a lot about your children and we value what you can tell us about them'. Equally we are saying to the children, 'We believe you know a lot about your learning; please tell us'.

Eva responds to her children's reports

One parent, Eva, told us what happens in her house now when one of her children brings home a report. 'To begin with,' she said, 'I have three children, and this style of reporting means that we only ever get one report at a time. This gives us more time to spend with each child when a report comes home.' She went on to tell us how she reads the report quickly when it's given to her, and then after tea sits down with the child and the report and they read it together. They talk about it and together decide on the response. This is just one way in which negotiated evaluation helps support family links and creates opportunities for interaction between parent and child.

Parent observation profiles

The teachers at Nareena Hills devised parent observation profiles with the help of information I supplied from British Columbia. The purpose of these profiles was to involve parents in observing their children more keenly, and to support and assist them in developing their understanding of the aspects of learning the school particularly valued. Samples of lower primary sheets are shown in Figures 4.1–4.5.

My Son as a Language Learner	
Please indicate your observations of your son's reading in the following areas.	
1. My son likes me to read to him (e.g. he brings home books from the school library to share; likes regular bedtime stories).	
2. My son reads stories to me (e.g. shares stories he has read at school; reads or attempts to read his own library books).	
3. My son attempts to read in everyday situations (e.g. street signs; store signs; cereal boxes).	
4. My son can retell a story so that I can understand it (e.g. retells a story heard at school; retells a story to brother, sister, friend).	
5. My son figures out new words he sees (e.g. uses meaning clues and letter-sounds to read a store or street sign; perseveres in figuring out unknown words in a story).	
6. When my son reads he 'guesses' at words but they usually make sense in the story (e.g. the story might say 'John was racing home' but he might read 'John was running home').	

Figure 4.1

My Daughter as a Language Learner	
Please indicate your observations of your daughter's writing in the following areas.	
1. My daughter voluntarily engages in independent drawing and writing activities.	
2. My daughter likes to talk about or display her drawing and writing.	
3. My daughter uses writing to send messages to others.	
4. My daughter will try out new words on her own.	
5. Others are increasingly able to read what my daughter writes.	

Figure 4.2

Justine makes good use of the parent profiles

Justine, who had just moved into a new house and was very proud of it, wouldn't allow her son Alfie to put up his work anywhere as it would upset the new decor. Although she had been a teacher herself, she had forgotten how important it can be for children to display their work at home — that is, until she read about it on the parent profile sheet sent from school. It was from her response to this profile that we learnt of the situation. The classroom teacher suggested that a solution might be to put up a noticeboard in Alfie's room. Several days later Alfie reported to his teacher that he was now the proud owner of a brand-new noticeboard and could put up all his work on it in his room.

My Son and Mathematics Please indicate your observations of your son's activities in mathematics in the following areas.	
1. My son recognises numbers in everyday situations.	
2. My son likes to help me with the cooking and often measures out ingredients to help.	
3. My son asks for tasks involving numbers (e.g. measuring, counting, sums).	
4. My son often includes numbers as part of his play (e.g. playing shops or schools).	
5. My son shows ability to think logically and solve problems.	
6. My son uses language to communicate mathematical concepts (e.g. more than, in front of, behind, etc.).	

Figure 4.3

An explanatory letter was sent out with the first profile about six weeks after the whole program began.

Dear Parents,

We hope that you have been enjoying the first report on your child's progress and have found it useful in assisting his learning at home.

With this note there is an observation profile that we'd like you to complete. It has some guidelines that should help you think

My Daughter and School	
1. My daughter enjoys going to school.	
2. My daughter likes to talk about things that happen at school.	
3. My daughter plays well both as an individual and in a group.	
4. My daughter readily accepts respon-sibility (e.g. completes chores; takes care of her own belongings).	

Figure 4.4

about your son as a 'reader' and a 'writer'. Please comment on anything you've noticed about him that you think we may not know.

Please send it back by 23rd March.

Our sincere thanks

_____   _____

(Principal)   (Teacher)

The most interesting feature of the completed profiles turned out to be the section in which parents were asked to tell the teacher something they had noticed about their child that they thought the teacher would not know (Figure 4.5). This proved to be very valuable, since through it teachers not only got to know more about the children in their class, but were also able to watch the growth in parents' understanding of their child's learning.

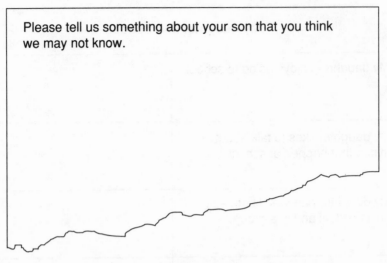

Please tell us something about your son that you think
we may not know.

Figure 4.5

When parents returned the profiles to the school, the sheets were placed in the child's report folder so that they would go home again each time a report was sent. It was reasoned that this would encourage parents to revisit their observations and comments and allow them to see the progress made. It would also act as a reminder of their role as observers.

As with other procedures associated with negotiated evaluation, school staffs with whom I have worked have each devised their own parent profiles. Some have worked as a whole staff to devise a profile to cover all grades, some have worked at each grade level, while others have devised one profile for lower primary (K–Year 2), one for middle primary (Years 3 & 4), and one for upper primary (Years 5 & 6).

Parent reports

The attempt to make parents more aware of their children's progress was reinforced later, after several cycles of focused observation had produced several reports, by sending them an open report sheet accompanied by their child's report folder. The sheets had spaces for remarks on reading, writing, maths, other curriculum areas and relationships/ attitudes. Parents were asked to read back through the reports, their comments and the child's comments and then to write about the progress they felt their child had made. It was emphasised that this should be done in collaboration with the child.

Communication books

In some schools with which I have had contact, only one teacher, rather than the entire staff, has decided to try negotiated evaluation in his or her classroom. Parent profiles and reporting mechanisms devised and developed on a school-wide basis were clearly inappropriate in these circumstances. Instead, one teacher devised a 'communication book' for each child. Rather than writing a report at the end of a focused observation period, she wrote her comments in an exercise book. These books she sent home on a continuous basis, asking parents to reply. They found the books most informative and were more than willing to respond. This once again demonstrates what can happen when teachers give parents the invitation, opportunity and space to respond honestly to a report, especially if there is a clear expectation that a reply is wanted and valued.

Involving parents of NESB children

Schools with a high proportion of students from non-English speaking backgrounds face a challenge in communicating with parents at any time, and introducing negotiated evaluation is no exception.

The first step is to ascertain the preferred written language of the parents. While some parents may read and write in a language other than English, others may prefer communications to be sent home in English, so that they can get them translated by a friend or neighbour. If they are not literate in their first language, it could be highly embarrassing to have to ask someone to read it to them, but getting English translated carries no stigma.

Some children may act as translators for their parents, particularly older children. Naturally the child translator is then aware of the contents of the communication, but in negotiated evaluation this is expected and can help to consolidate and extend the interaction between the child and teacher and the child and parents.

When a significant number of parents share a common cultural and language background, they or the school can arrange a meeting with the teacher and a translator. The translator can help the teacher to explain orally the process of negotiated evaluation and, if necessary, can translate and clarify the reports.

Tape-recorded communications can also help in crossing language barriers. Instead of written reports or other communications, tape recordings are sent home. Written versions can accompany the tapes, so that parents have some permanent record to keep if they wish.

As for communication from home to school, my experience is that once parents have appreciated the importance the school is placing on their involvement in the evaluation process, most have found ways of completing profiles and responding to reports with the help of an interpreter or their children.

Conclusion

The main priority when involving parents in their children's evaluation is to assure them that we value what they know and that we will support them in developing their understanding of the learning process. If this is done, the responses from parents will serve the needs of both teachers and children. When parents have a better understanding of their children's learning, they can be of more help to them. Stronger links will be forged between parents and their children as they collaborate in learning, and teachers will be supported more effectively in what they attempt in classrooms. Surely education and society can only benefit from such a process.

CHAPTER FIVE

The Children's Role

One of the most important features of negotiated evaluation is the involvement of the children who are being evaluated. It is brought about in two ways: the teacher continually interacts with each child during the focused observation periods, and children learn how to evaluate themselves. The teacher's interaction with individual children has already been discussed in Chapter 3, and so this chapter will concentrate on children's self-evaluation.

Why is self-evaluation important?

Given time and support, children can develop the capacity to evaluate themselves. There are many things they know which can add to what parents and teachers know. There are some things that only they really know about themselves. They know what they believe and feel. They know what they know. They know what they understand. There is no test that can tell you all these things about each and every child, and even the best and closest system of observation will not reveal everything.

There are four main reasons why self-evaluation is so important:

1   Only the participant (the learner) knows the full extent of the enjoyment, understanding and interaction experienced during any activity.

2   Children have the right to contribute to knowledge gathered about their progress and to have access to the expectations held by other interested parties.

3   Giving children more control and responsibility for what they do through self-evaluation and goal-setting fosters the development

of skills for independent life-long learning. It also makes them more aware of their own learning processes.

4   Teachers are always conscious of the time constraints placed on them in the classroom and should therefore be prepared to transfer to children as many evaluation tasks as possible.

There are quite a number of strategies that will encourage children to participate in their own evaluation, including logs, learning journals, portfolios, evaluation books, self-evaluation sheets and child-led conferences. The rest of this chapter is devoted to describing and discussing these strategies.

Logs

A log is the simplest form of self-evaluation, as it is basically a record of some activity completed. The most obvious and popular self-evaluation logs are those kept for reading and writing, but they can be of use in any curriculum area where records need to be kept about work in progress and work completed. There is little point in having logs, however, if you do not give children an opportunity to fill them in. Sufficient time should be aside towards the end of a session for children to evaluate what they have achieved and complete their logs.

Reading logs

In reading logs children are usually asked to record such things as the author, title and type of books they have begun, and whether or not they have finished reading them. Many teachers also ask for a comment of some kind.

Initially children may simply record the author and title of a book and the date it was read (Figure 5.1). At this stage they may need to ask for assistance from a more advanced 'buddy' or a parent helper to complete their logs. Alternatively small, self-adhesive labels, computer printed with the titles and authors of books in the classroom, can be made available, either in a pocket at the back of each book or in a central position.

At the next stage children can add the genre of the book and enter the dates of starting and finishing their reading. Finally they should be able to add comments on each of the books they have read and any activity they may have completed (Figure 5.2).

The information contained in these logs gives the teacher an insight into each child's preferences, behaviours and understandings about reading. It also helps child and teacher to keep track of books read,

BOOKS I HAVE READ		
Name *Mary*		
Date read	Title	Author
7 May	*Who Sank the Boat?*	*Pamela Allen*
9 May	*Dinosaurs (pop-up)*	*—*

Figure 5.1 *Beginning reading log*

READING LOG Name *Jimmy*				
Date(s)	Title/Author	What I think about this book	Activity	Type
9/10–17/10	*Cannily, Cannily by Simon French*	*Realistic as to what happens with some kids and their family and teacher*	*Letter from Trevor to Martin*	*realistic fiction*
15/10–20/10	*Skateboard by Russ Howell*	*Out of date but still some good information*	*Yes!*	*'how to' book*

Figure 5.2 *Proficient reading log*

JOSEPH

1. NUMBER OF BOOKS READ COMPLETELY: *14*

2. TYPES –
   FICTION: *2*
   NON-FICTION: *5*
   PICTURE BOOKS: *3*
   POETRY: *4*

3. NUMBER OF BOOKS NOT COMPLETED: *2*

4. MOST FAVOURITE BOOK READ:
   Sister Madge's Book of Nuns (Poetry)

   AUTHOR:
   Doug Macleod

5. WHY I ENJOYED IT:
   I liked it because of the comedy, the action and the rhymes.

6. COMMENTS ON MY READING PROGRESS:
   I think my reading progress is kind of good.

7. MY TEACHER'S COMMENTS:
   Joseph, I'm very pleased with your reading too. I would like you to try some fiction books for some variety. Get one you'll be really interested in - how about trying 'Deezle Boy', a story about a boy your age who is crazy about trains, especially diesel trains?

Figure 5.3 *Collaborative reading evaluation sheet*

activities undertaken and the appropriateness of these activities to the book read. Initially the comments made by children about what they have read may seem fairly shallow, but with practice they will be able to make more informed comments that will help the teacher to evaluate their level of comprehension and the type of books they enjoy.

Having a record of the genres a child is reading allows teacher and child to note the range being sampled. It can reveal possible interests and expose gaps in the child's reading profile. This kind of record can be compiled through a process known as collaborative evaluation.

Collaborative evaluation

According to Hancock (1992), children should be responsible for collating the information from their reading logs under various headings on a reading evaluation sheet (Figure 5.3). The number of completed books and their genre or type are noted, along with the number of books not completed. The purpose of counting the books is not to induce competition but to reveal the reader's patterns of choice. This provides a valuable base for discussion and helps teacher, parents or peers to make suggestions about other books that might be read. Hancock reports that the process of collating information for the evaluation sheet not only makes children reflect about their reading patterns but can also surprise them with a realisation of their achievements.

Writing logs

Writing logs are kept for similar reasons as reading logs (though it must be remembered that they are records of what has been achieved, not of the quality of either process or product). Once children begin to understand the writing process, they are capable of keeping a writing log. Initially they might record the date and title of a piece of writing, later adding the genre (Figure 5.4). As they progress, their logs can be extended to include conferencing points and processes completed (Figure 5.5). This helps the teacher to keep an eye on issues discussed in individual conferences and monitor the range of processes and genres each child is using. It helps children to keep track of what they have done and reminds them of expectations their teacher has voiced at conferences. As with reading, collaborative evaluation sheets can be used to collate writing log information and stimulate further discussion between teacher and child (Figure 5.6).

Learning journals

Another kind of self-evaluation tool is the learning journal, which requires children to reflect and enter comments about what they have learnt, what they know and what they want to know. However, we should not expect them to be able to write a journal at the drop of a hat; it is an

WRITING LOG		
Name *Peter*		
Date	Title	Genre
4/3	*My Birthday*	*Recount*
5/3	*Ghosts*	*Story*

Figure 5.4 *Beginning writing log*

WRITING LOG			
Name *Elizabeth*			
Title	Genre	Processes and dates	Conferencing points
Letter to local council	*Business letter*	*1st draft 2/6* *Editing 3/6* *2nd draft 4/6* *Publishing 5/6*	*Letter format*

Figure 5.5 *Advanced writing log*

AISHA

1. NUMBER OF PIECES OF WRITING
    COMPLETED: *12*

2. TYPES –
    NARRATIVE: *3*
    EXPOSITORY: *5*
    LETTERS: *2*
    REPORTS: *2*
    DESCRIPTION: *1*
    POETRY: *4*

3. NUMBER OF PIECES NOT COMPLETED: *7*

4. MY FAVOURITE PIECE:
    The Ghost Story

5. WHY I ENJOYED IT:
    I was able to create an atmosphere of spookiness by using really spooky words.

6. COMMENTS ON MY WRITING PROGRESS:
    I'm OK in narratives but I need some help in reports.

7. MY TEACHER'S COMMENTS:
    I'm very pleased with your narratives too. You are able to create interesting images in the reader's head. For your reports you need to check the specific words and phrases that make a report more readable.

Figure 5.6 *Collaborative writing evaluation sheet*

acquired skill that needs a lot of oral preparation. The first step is to program some sessions in which children share their ideas about what they have learnt and how they have accomplished tasks — this will help them put their thinking into words. The ideas that emerge in these sessions can then be consolidated and put in writing by the teacher as she demonstrates the processes of journal writing to the class.

If you do include journal writing in your daily routine, don't forget to allow adequate time for it in class. Eventually you should aim to encourage children to add notes of follow-up action at the end of their journal entries — for example:

2.6.92

Today I learned about air. I didn't know that a fire uses oxygen to burn. I saw a plan on how to use the air to help make a paper helicopter work. I will look it up and see what happens and if it works.

Notes can also take the form of goals children wish to set for themselves, and later on in the journal they can evaluate what they have learnt in terms of these goals.

As long as the information contained in journals is used, so that children can see a purpose in keeping them, and as long as they are not perceived as threatening or a chore, they can become an important and valid evaluation tool shared between child and teacher. Periods of focused observation may be the most convenient time to review and discuss the journals of each focus group.

To add impetus to the process, teachers should consider keeping learning journals themselves. As well as being shared at times with children (which will encourage them to keep up their own), they can be genuinely useful as self-evaluation tools.

Portfolios

'Portfolio' seems to be one of the buzz words in evaluation, particularly in North America. However, everyone who uses the term seems to have a different idea of the content and purpose of a portfolio. While I have no wish to create yet another definition or to claim that there is only one way to go about using portfolios, it does seem to me time for some of these ideas and definitions to be drawn together.

The Manchester project in New Hampshire, where portfolios are used throughout the school system (with a particular emphasis on literacy), provides us with one perspective. Another comes in the shape of the process-files used in an art class at Schenley High School in Pittsburgh. Both these examples warrant examination so that we can take a wider view of record keeping and individual evaluation through portfolios.

Literacy portfolios in New Hampshire

The main purpose of portfolios in the Manchester project (Hansen 1992) was for the children each to discover what it meant to them to be a literate person. To this end they collected a variety of items that helped to describe themselves and their literacy development. The kind of items included were work samples, photos, certificates of achievement, photocopies of covers of favourite books, and writing about events, experiences or feelings.

The teachers and researchers also developed portfolios of their own, not only so that they could find out more about their own literacy development, but also to demonstrate the portfolio process to the children.

One important feature of this project was the requirement that portfolios should include a justification for the choice of each item. This helped the compilers to articulate their thinking and gave more substance to their work. (The comments of beginning writers were scribed on post-its by the teacher or a helper for the child to stick on the relevant item.) As portfolios developed, progress over time became evident, both in the quality of the contents and in comment about it.

Although the literacy portfolio was classed as an evaluation item, no grades were given for it. More to the point were teacher-child conferences during which questions were asked about the contents of the portfolio to help clarify and refine the ideas of the owner. One of the main outcomes of the project was an improvement in the children's self-esteem, and of course the additional information about each child helped support the teacher's planning for individual development.

Another advantage of these portfolios was that they were shared with a variety of people. The children shared them at school with their peers and at home with their parents, which gave each family a sense of what was important to their child. People who saw the portfolios were asked to comment positively on a response sheet (Figure 5.7). These responses not only provided the children with useful feedback on their choice of items but also helped to confirm their own perception of their literacy, as well as increasing their self-esteem.

Process-folios

Zessoules and Gardner (1991) describe process-folios as 'selected works showing the development of students' learning over time', and though they developed the idea in the context of a secondary school art class, it could easily be adapted to any curriculum area of a primary school. The process-folios they describe contained a range of work selected for both

PORTFOLIO RESPONSE SHEET

Name *Jasper*

Parent Response

I liked	because
the maths game	*it showed how you solve problems*
the letter to the council	*you argued your point very well*
your drawing	*because the colours used for the trees were very subtle*

Peer Response

I liked	because
your story about camping	*it had really good words*
the science experiment	*I didn't know that leaves were so important to trees*

Figure 5.7

variety and quality, which revealed the depth, breadth and growth of the student's thinking. Admissible items included notes, detailed studies, journal excerpts telling the story of the development of specific ideas and actual pieces of work. According to Zessoules and Gardner, these process-folios 'sample the terrain' covered by the student and have the potential to provide an even richer opportunity for learning and evaluation because they are intended to document the evolution of new understandings over time and across many experiences — both satisfying and unsatisfying.

Clearly portfolios may take different forms and have different purposes, but they are now seen by many as an alternative to tests, since they give a clearer picture of the owner's development. A portfolio is, I believe, the child's record, not only of progress but of what he or she considers to be important. The use of portfolios therefore provides the teacher with another perspective on the child's thinking.

Evaluation books

Some schools involved in negotiated evaluation use special books to help children collect evaluation material. These evaluation books can be used in a variety of ways. For example, during their week of focused observation children work in their evaluation book, completing in it their writing, maths, science and so on. The teacher then has an easily accessible collection of the current work of the children being focused on. An added advantage is that the book can be taken home to show parents what work their child is doing. And, of course, by the end of the year it provides an excellent record of the progress its owner has made during the year.

A similar self-evaluation tool, called an 'assessment book', is described by Fryar, Johnston and Leaker (1992). This book is used to store a great deal of assessment information. It includes a letter from the teacher to the child and his or her parents, child-set goals, logs, conference notes and other self-evaluation information, including weekly and term reviews of what the individual has accomplished. I see the use of such assessment books as being extremely valuable, particularly when integrated with the processes of negotiated evaluation. The comfortable 'fit' here is that while these books are a regular and well-used feature of the classroom, they too can be focused on during the week their owners are the subject of focused observation, providing an added, accurate, convenient and child-centred source of information about each child, from the child's own perspective.

Self-evaluation sheets

My experience of observing children filling out self-evaluation sheets (Figures 5.8–5.10) indicates that they can evaluate themselves very competently. Whether or not sheets are to be completed without help will obviously depend on a child's reading ability and the level of difficulty of the concepts involved, but it may also depend on the teacher's wish to spend this time with the child so as to better understand his or her thinking processes. Even if the sheet is completed privately, the teacher may still need to discuss some responses to clarify what the child is thinking. After all, if there is any room for doubt, it is always unwise to make assumptions about what a child is thinking.

What do you feel about reading?

The things I like to read are

My reading would improve if

What do you feel about writing?

The things I like about writing are

My writing would improve if

Figure 5.8 *English self-evaluation sheet*

How do you feel in maths at the moment? Circle the appropriate word:

interested   relaxed   worried   successful   confused   clever   happy
bored   rushed

Write down one word of your own about maths.

Maths activities I enjoy doing are

My maths would improve if

Figure 5.9   *Maths self-evaluation sheet*

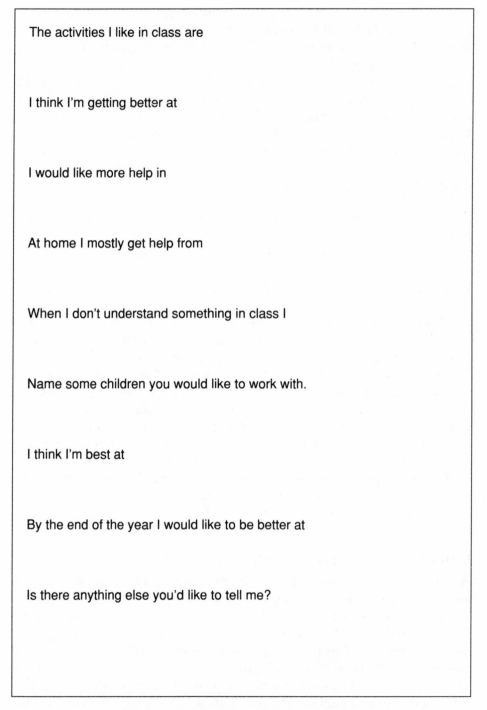

The activities I like in class are

I think I'm getting better at

I would like more help in

At home I mostly get help from

When I don't understand something in class I

Name some children you would like to work with.

I think I'm best at

By the end of the year I would like to be better at

Is there anything else you'd like to tell me?

Figure 5.10   *General self-evaluation sheet*

The examples of self-evaluation sheets come from St Bernadette's School, Castle Hill, NSW. A story attached to them concerns a child who answered the last question on the general sheet (Figure 5.10) by saying 'Yes, I can't hear you'. Was she was asking the teacher to speak up, we wondered, or was she trying to say 'I have a hearing problem'? To resolve doubts, the school and parents cooperated to organise a full auditory assessment, which revealed a chronic hearing loss. A story like this certainly reinforces the argument for children being able to participate fully in evaluation procedures.

Child-led conferences

The final self-evaluation tool to be discussed here is the child-led conference. A child-led conference is a conference between a parent and child, controlled and organised by the child (Anthony et al. 1992). It is both a natural progression from and synthesis of the self-evaluation procedures already reviewed, and is a useful adjunct to the parent-teacher interview.

Although some schools have tried to include the child in a parent-teacher interview, even changing the name from 'interview' to 'conference', I believe that little of the context of such interviews has altered. The child is still peripheral to the discussion and the position of power still lies with the teacher. A child-led conference changes all this. Yet though the conference is child-led and child-centred, the teacher's role behind the scenes remains important. The preparatory organisation of portfolios and daily routines is crucial, as is the teacher's drawing together of the child's future directions after the conference.

The account of child-led conferences which follows is based on observations I made of Dianne Cowden's first grade class in British Columbia, in collaboration with Alison Preece.

Children's and teacher's preparation

A child-led conference begins with the children currently involved in focused observation gathering samples of their work, either as part of their portfolio or in addition to it. They select from these samples items that they believe will show their progress or are 'favourite' pieces, for whatever reason. The idea is for them to each deliberate on what is important to them educationally and to explain that importance to their parents. To be able to do this, they first of all need to sit down with a peer or friend and explain why they selected the various items and what these items show about their learning. At the same time they should also

A friend's questions about your portfolio can help you
clarify the reasons for your choice.

articulate some goals they wish to achieve. The teacher may feel a need
to be part of this interaction initially, but the more responsibility can be
left with the children, the more ownership they will feel.

In addition to supervising the building of portfolios, the teacher
needs to prepare some observation sheets like the one illustrated in
Figure 5.11. (Separate 'he' and 'she' sheets should be prepared for boys
and girls, as they seem more personalised and less awkward in their
wording than one gender-inclusive sheet.) The sheets are for parents to
record observations on while watching their children in normal classroom activities, prior to the child-led conference. The main aim of the
questions is to focus the parent on the learning behaviours of the child
rather than on his or her academic achievements. There is no suggestion of comparison — the focus is on the one child only.

A letter is sent home asking parents to say on which morning they will
be able to come to the school for a conference. It is anticipated that at
least one parent from each family will be able to come (only one family
will be represented on any one morning). In the Canadian school in
which I first saw this idea in operation, the response from parents was
one hundred per cent.

PARENT OBSERVATION SHEET

Please observe your daughter and write your observations in the space provided.

– How does your daughter interact with others? What does she do during group work/whole class activity/individual work?

– What is her attitude to class work? Does she seem to enjoy what she is doing? Does she have difficulty in settling down to the task at hand?

– What surprises have you discovered about your daughter?

– What is something special that you have noticed about her today?

– How does she solve any problems that may have arisen?

– What decisions did she make today? How easy was it for her to make those decisions?

Figure 5.11

On the day

Parents come into the classroom for the first session to observe their child in action. This is intended as a means of enhancing the child-parent relationship. As the parents will be in your classroom for the entire early morning session, you should look closely at the activities you have planned and ensure that the child being observed is actively

A Year 2 child leads his mother through items from his portfolio

engaged. I would also recommend that 'daily news' or 'show and tell' not be part of your plan.

Parents sit close by their child with their observation sheet and record their observations over a period of thirty to forty-five minutes. After this, the child takes his or her parent(s) and portfolio to a quiet corner of the room (the writing corner, for example) and goes through it, explaining why the items have been included and how each relates to his or her learning and personal goals. Parents are of course free to ask questions and make comments. This section of the conference should last up to recess time. During recess, over a cup of coffee (and some juice, milk or soft drink for the child) teacher and parent(s) discuss their vision for the child for the rest of the school year. The child is included and the goals he or she has set are incorporated in the discussion, which lasts about fifteen minutes at most.

Parents I have met who had been involved in this type of conference were delighted with the amount of information they had gained about their children and were comfortable in the knowledge that they now had some input into their education. The 'vision' they expressed for their children was interesting — most did not emphasise academic aspects (for example, 'to be a better reader') but focused more on social learning (for example, 'to be a better person', 'to communicate', 'to get along with others').

Conclusion

As can be seen from the various examples of self-evaluation tools included in this chapter, there are many opportunities for the children in your classroom to be part of their own evaluation. Moreover, if children are to reach their ultimate potential as responsible, self-directed learners, it is important for them to feel that they *are* an integral part of the evaluation processes that occur in their classroom.

CHAPTER SIX

Interpreting Evaluation Data

We have already discussed some of the roles the teacher plays in negotiated evaluation (those of observer, collector of data, organiser and negotiator) and seen that one result is the collection of a large amount of information. Now what happens to this information? Does it just get added to the pile collected previously? Or does it get used? In that case, how can it best be used to assist the teacher in making decisions of merit and worth and in planning for the future? How can it be used to inform learning? In this chapter I hope to answer these questions.

Consider this scenario. It is week 6 of Term 1 and Graham, a Year 1/2 teacher at a large primary school in an NSW country town, has been focusing on five children for five days. He has observed each child in a variety of circumstances and in all the key learning areas, and has recorded these observations in writing. He has also collected samples of each child's work, dated them and looked at them carefully. He has made some decisions — not only about the quality of each work sample but also about the progress that has been made since he last checked samples of work from these children five weeks ago. He has written appropriate comments at the bottom or on the back of each sample.

Graham has also made sure that during the focus period he has taken the time to speak with each of the children, discussing with them some points of interest and perhaps areas of concern. He has recorded what was discussed and filed his comments with his records of observation. He has also collected the children's self-evaluations and the parent profile sheets.

Now what does he do with all this information?

One of the first things he does is to analyse it and document this analysis. 'Analysis' simply means looking at the information you have, determining its essential features, making decisions about its quality and documenting the decisions in some recognisable and usable form. Graham has already begun this process through the decisions he has made about the samples of work, and now he needs to continue it with the rest of the information he has collected. The simplest way for him to document his decisions is to write them down, perhaps in the form of a small report.

Graham understands the benefit of writing down what he discovers as he pulls together the understandings he has developed in the course of a careful review of the information he has collected. He realises that he's not just writing a report to satisfy the school's requirements for reporting to parents, or to provide information to the children and the parents (although they will be the ultimate audience for his analysis). He is writing a report for himself in the first instance, in order to consolidate his understanding of each child's development so that he can make informed decisions as he plans for their learning.

Clearly the next step for Graham is to send a summary of his analysis to the parents of the five children — after consultation with the children of course, for, as we have seen, the child is integral to the evaluation process and needs to be included all along the way. The nature of this report to parents will be descriptive, perhaps in point form, but grades and scores will not play any part in it.

In summary, then, Graham needs to document his analysis of collected information for the following reasons:

- to draw together the salient points

- to consolidate the information in written form in order to facilitate making decisions about each child and his or her learning

- to inform both child and parents at the earliest possible point in the school year of each child's progress, and to continue to keep them informed

- to encourage both parents and children to be part of the reporting process by providing them with regular reports to which they are encouraged to respond (see Chapter 4)

- to have a demonstrable record of each child's progress over time

- to demonstrate that he is being professionally responsible to and for the children in his care.

Because Graham is focusing on a particular group of five children this week, he will be sending reports home to the parents of these five at the end of the week. Next week he will focus on another five children and will send their reports home at the end of that week, and so the cycle will continue. This means that each family should receive four to six reports a year. The reports are not long and involved, but contain specific descriptions of what the child can do and what work he or she has completed. They also feature a section recommending how the parents can help their child 'get to the next step'.

You may consider this side of negotiated evaluation (the collection of the data, its analysis and the writing of the reports) slightly overwhelming, but please consider again the following points:

- never again will you have to 'front up' to thirty reports (at any one point there are only ever five to write)

- the children in your care will more clearly understand their learning and your teaching

- you will come to know each child in a way you never thought possible

- your teaching will change as it becomes more closely attuned to the current needs of children

- parents will have more accurate information about their children at an earlier stage in the school year, and more frequently throughout the year

- parents will be more aware of their children's progress.

Have I convinced you? Well if I have, it's time to show you how to get from data collection to final documentation in the form of a descriptive report. To illustrate the process, I have chosen one of Graham's pupils, Richard, a seven-year-old. He is one of eight Year 2 children in Graham's composite class, which also includes twenty-one Year 1 children.

Data analysis

During his week-long observations of Richard and four other children Graham has collected data from all key learning areas. For this reporting period, however, he has decided to focus his observations specifically on the areas of English, Maths and the Creative and Practical Arts. He focuses on English and Maths every time he collects data and adds one of the other key learning areas each focus period, systematically working through all parts of the curriculum.

In order to draw his observations together, he has chosen to categorise them under the headings of risk-taking, responsibility, collaboration, knowledge, creativity, learning strategies, inquiry and industry.

He has selected these categories because he considers them important characteristics for seven-year-olds to develop, and finds they help him achieve greater depth in his analysis of information.

For ease of distribution he has recorded his observations on small post-its (Figures 6.1a, 6.1b and 6.2), using his own form of shorthand. This means that the notes aren't necessarily decipherable to an outsider, but they aren't intended to be — they are for Graham alone, and it is only at the reporting stage that he must ensure that what he has written is suitable for the intended audience.

20/6
- gets down to work
  immediately
- takes breaks from time
  to time
- takes risks in word
  development
- finishes quickly
- not willing to extend
  his work

20/6
- understands strategy of
  re-reading and reading on in
  order to find out unknown
  words, but still uses
  'sounding out' as first
  line of action

21/6
- had difficulty when reading
  with word 'ferocious';
  accepted another child's
  suggestion of 'furry' as
  it made sense in context

21/6
- came back to 'ferocious'
  and tried 'fearsome'
- re-read 'ferocious' to
  himself during big
  book session

Figure 6.1a *Graham's observations of Richard over the first two days*

2216
- joined in reading of big
  book word by word
- enthusiastic
- very engrossed
- confident

2216
- uses picture clues
- combines meaning-based
  strategies and sounding
  out
- phonics sometimes get
  in the way of meaning,
  especially with names
- can settle to task but
  easily distracted; anxious
  to participate in class
  activities

2316
- at ease with telling
  the time
- knows o'clock, 1/2 past,
  1/2x60=30
- can take turns, count
  backwards
- has well-developed concepts
  of size, temperature and
  volume in response to
  worksheets

2416
- helps others with their
  work and accepts
  assistance
- very precise with colouring
- has difficulty with
  pattern-copying but is
  not concerned
- loses himself in his work
  when he is painting
- not afraid to use his
  imagination

Figure 6.1b *Graham's observations of Richard over the last three days*

As Graham distributes the information into the categories he has selected, it begins to look like this.

Risk taking

Takes risks in word development. Not willing to extend written work.

Had difficulty with 'ferocious'. Accepted another child's suggestion of 'furry' as it made sense in context. Came back to this word later and tried 'fearsome'. Re-read 'ferocious' to himself during big book.

> 23/6
> - likes science best of all
> - he is inquisitive and wants
>   to know how things work
>   and how to make things
> - would like to work more
>   with 'toys and stuff'
>   in maths
> - reads at home
> - doesn't write at home

Figure 6.2   *Comments recorded after a discussion with Richard*

Responsibility

Gets down to work immediately.

Helps others with their work.

Collaboration

Accepted another child's suggestion.

Can take turns.

Helps others with their work and accepts assistance.

Knowledge

At ease with telling the time — knows o'clock, 1/2 past, 1/2 x 60 = 30. Can take turns, count backwards. Has well-developed concepts of size, temperature and volume in response to work sheets.

Creativity

Loses himself in his work when he is painting. Not afraid to use his imagination.

Learning strategies

Understands strategy of re-reading and reading on in order to find out unknown words, but uses 'sounding out' as first line of action.

Uses picture clues; combines meaning-based strategies and sounding out,

6/6
Richard likes to retell stories at home but does not write willingly. He becomes engrossed in reading 'how it works' type books. Still likes to be read to sometimes. Has lots of friends over to play with him.

Figure 6.3 *Comments recorded by parent on parent-profile sheet*

though phonics sometimes get in the way of meaning, especially with names. Can 'accurately' retell.

Inquiry

Likes science best of all. He is inquisitive and wants to know how things work and how to make things.

Industry

Gets down to work immediately — takes breaks from time to time.

Finishes quickly.

Joined in reading of big book word by word — enthusiastic — very engrossed — confident.

Can settle to task but easily distracted.

Anxious to participate in class activities.

Richard's report

Once Graham has categorised his observations, he is ready to write his report. This report, reproduced below, will be useful to him in making programming decisions about directions he might take with Richard over the next few weeks, and it will of course be shared with Richard and his parents.

Richard is becoming a strong risk-taker, which is important in learning. He experiments with words when he is writing as he strives towards conventional spelling. He continues to attempt to work out unknown words, aiming always to make sense of what he is reading. However, he needs to be more adventurous when writing by endeavouring to extend and improve each piece of his writing. Richard and I will be working to achieve this in the coming weeks.

Richard shows responsibility towards his work as he usually gets down to work immediately, although he can be easily distracted at times. He is willing to help others with their work and is able to do this appropriately. He co-operates well with others in a collaborative manner as he accepts help from others and is able to take turns. Richard has many friends and is able to socialise effectively with them.

In maths he is able to apply his knowledge of time in appropriate situations and has established some concepts of size, temperature and volume.

Richard is creative in his drawing and makes good use of his imagination in both art and writing. He understands that reading is a meaning-making process as he re-reads and reads on when he comes to unknown words. He uses picture clues and is beginning to combine meaning-making with sounding-out strategies.

Richard works well most of the time. He is confident in reading and maths and is eager to participate in class activities.

You can help Richard by encouraging him to continue to seek meaning first when reading and to use 'sounding out' only as a confirmation of the meaning he has predicted. He also needs practical experience in under-standing the relationships between objects of different volume, e.g. litre, 500ml, 250ml. We should foster his interest in science as he has much to offer others in this area.

Graham Roberts
Teacher

The term 'risk-taking' may be one that Richard's parents are unfamiliar with as a positive educational attribute, and so Graham attempts to explain it in his report and show its value in regard to Richard's learning. Before this report goes home, Richard will have an opportunity to read it and query any comments or add anything he feels has been omitted.

The next report should show the progress Richard has made since this one was written. In it Graham will try to establish the meaning and relevance of another characteristic (for example, 'responsibility') and will extend the issues raised in this report.

Making decisions

How does Graham move from the analysis recorded in this report to the decisions that will inform Richard's learning? The first step is to look at Richard's areas of need, and then at how his strengths might be extended. Graham records his thoughts on a sheet to go in Richard's file.

RICHARD'S NEEDS (24/6/92)

1) *He needs help to extend his written work*

   - *Serialise a book to show that work on one piece can continue for several days.*

   - *Authors' circle.*

   - *Demonstrate to whole class how extending their writing can lead to improved quality.*

2) *He is easily distracted*

   Observe when and where distractions occur. Are there any patterns, e.g. does it always occur in writing? The appropriateness of task may be an issue here.

3) *Mathematics*

   He needs more work on the practical application of measurement. I need to give some thought to re-organising my maths program so that the children will have greater access to hands-on experiences regularly and not just exercises about them.

4) *Interest in science*

   Richard could help set up science situations for other children to solve. I will need to ask him about this and see what he comes up with.

As you can see, there are several strands in Graham's decisions. One suggests individual work to be done with Richard, another further observations that need to be made. There is a need too for extension of and a change in teaching practices, and for consultation with Richard as to how he might further develop his strengths.

Because you will be focusing on at least five children at a time, not just one, many of the decisions you make will be about groups of children as specific needs and strengths emerge, and you will discover similarities across your class that will allow you to form groups based on these needs and strengths.

Comments on the report

Before the report is sent home, Graham takes the time to sit down quietly with Richard and share it with him. After he has read it out, Richard comments on the part about science and says he will give it some thought. On the back of the report he pencils another comment:

I would like to write better pieces but I'm not sure how to yet.

Richard takes the report home to his parents. There is ample space for them to comment, which they do as follows:

We are pleased with Richard's progress at this stage of Year 2. We will continue to encourage him in his reading now that we know how we can help. Do you have any further suggestions about how we can help with his interest in science? Thank you.

With this type of negotiated evaluation and the ensuing interaction between teacher, parents and child, not only does each of the participants gain in knowledge and confidence, but learning becomes purposeful and more pertinent, and child, parents and teacher are all working towards a common goal.

CHAPTER SEVEN

Case Study

During the year in which I first piloted negotiated evaluation at Nareena Hills Public School, many other schools heard about the concept, showed great interest in it and decided to try it for themselves. One such school was Thomas Acres Public School.

Thomas Acres is a large, relatively new primary school in the south-west of Sydney. In 1990, when the school began its program of negotiated evaluation, there were 760 students, 27 class teachers and 2 support teachers. The school was initially housed at Rosemeadow Public School,

two kilometres away, until new premises were completed at the current site in 1986, and there is still some temporary accommodation in demountable buildings. Thomas Acres is in a rapidly growing area where the majority of parents work in trades. Over the past three or four years the school has made a constant effort to involve parents in the school's activities — with the usual solid core of parent workers strongly supporting the staff.

Getting started

My work at Thomas Acres began early in 1989 when I came in contact with the school in my capacity as a lecturer in Language Arts at the University of Western Sydney. I spoke with the executive and later with the district inspector about negotiated evaluation. An interest was shown, and executive staff, particularly the Deputy Principal, Steve Orton, then undertook a lot of reading and planning. I became involved in staff development for the lower primary teachers in the area of spelling, and this gave them the opportunity to try some focused observation, concentrating on specific aspects of children's spelling strategies.

At the end of 1989 all teachers in the lower primary grades carried out a series of focused observations on the children in their classes and then wrote a short report on each child (Figure 7.1). Around this time I was asked to take part in a meeting of the whole staff, where it was agreed that in 1990 the school would implement a program of negotiated evaluation on a voluntary basis. Eight of the twenty-seven class teachers showed an immediate interest, and by the beginning of 1990 twenty-two had decided to trial the program. Of course this necessitated a tremendous amount of organisation — in the form of further staff development, parent meetings, and the development of report proformas and parent profiles. To avoid conflict with the terminology of NSW Department of School Education policy, it was decided to adopt the term 'continuous assessment' instead of 'negotiated evaluation'.

Teething problems

At a staff meeting at the beginning of 1990, soon after the program had begun, it emerged that some difficulties were being experienced, and so a bulletin (Figure 7.2) was sent out to each member of staff involved in the program. The meeting that followed aimed to resolve some of these initial difficulties (it was the first of several such meetings held during the year to provide support and guidance for participating teachers). It was decided that there would be a minimum of four reports per year,

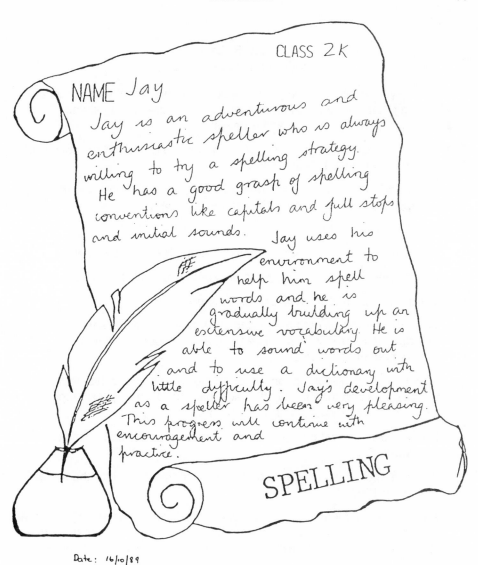

NAME Jay

Jay is an adventurous and enthusiastic speller who is always willing to try a spelling strategy. He has a good grasp of spelling conventions like capitals and full stops and initial sounds. Jay uses his environment to help him spell words and he is gradually building up an extensive vocabulary. He is able to sound words out and to use a dictionary with little difficulty. Jay's development as a speller has been very pleasing. This progress will continue with encouragement and practice.

CLASS 2K

SPELLING

Date: 16/10/89

Figure 7.1

with six being the ideal to aim for. The format for a sheet on which teachers could record their focused observations was discussed and it was decided that each teacher would be free to devise his or her own sheet. Some settled on one sheet for each child, while others preferred to have all six names on the one sheet. All decided to use curriculum areas for the headings on their observation sheets, instead of those initially adopted, which were 'attitude', 'processes', 'participation' and

Staff Bulletin
Evaluation Update 14/2/90

Following yesterday's meeting it has become apparent that some teachers are feeling that the workload for continuous assessment (negotiated evaluation) is too demanding and unrealistic.

At this early stage of the process your comments are vital to the success of the program and I value them highly.

I have talked to a number of teachers with different viewpoints and models, and it appears that a revision of the system may be needed.

Please keep in mind that:

- This is a voluntary method of assessment and reporting to parents.

- This is a well-researched model trialled both overseas and in Australia.

- We have Departmental and University support.

- This model gives us both a report to parents and an assessment system to include in our records. It will be the major component of your assessment of the children.

- If we reduce the reporting format to four per year and use this model, we will be doing less than many other schools who are giving term reports similar to our half-yearly and yearly reports.

- If you follow this system, you will not need to complete half-yearly and yearly reports.

- Assessment is the single area of emphasis for the school for the first six months of 1990.

- As this is a trial method in the school we will of course have problems that need to be sorted out as they arise. This is why next week's staff meeting is devoted entirely to focused observation. Please bring any of your reports to the meeting.

Teacher commitment to this system is an essential element in the trial.

See you at the staff meeting at 3.00 pm Tuesday.

Thanks —

Steve

Figure 7.2

'response'. While it was agreed these were laudable headings and would encourage cross-curriculum observations, the teachers had experienced a great deal of difficulty in using them when making and recording observations. As mentioned at the end of Chapter 3, it seems that coping with a new evaluation program was enough in itself, without the extra burden of coping with such broad headings for observations.

Additional support was given to participating teachers by the execut-ive, who secured funds to release a member of staff from classroom teaching for one day a week. This teacher would help others in making observations and gathering ideas for their reports, and would check what they had written so that further help could be provided where necessary. More staff meetings were organised to assist teachers in developing observation and evaluation strategies.

Involving parents

Initially two separate communications were sent home to parents. The first was a letter (Figure 7.3) informing parents of the new form of reporting that was to occur in their child's class, and the second was an invitation (Figure 7.4) to a parent meeting to discuss it, organised in early March before the first set of reports went home. At the meeting it was emphasised how much teachers valued parents' input into the program, which was explained more fully to them.

The information sent home to parents was adapted from that devel-oped in the pilot program at Nareena Hills Public School. It was felt that if the information was relatively brief, it would be more likely to gain parents' attention. The teachers at Thomas Acres also made some modi-fications to the program. In particular, they introduced open response sheets on which parents were encouraged to reply to reports (see Figure 7.8). These parent response sheets worked well and established a fur-ther line of communication between home and school.

One teacher decided to have a 'focus book' (a version of the 'evalu-ation book' discussed in Chapter 5). During any week the children who were being focused on would complete all their written work in their 'focus book', which would then accompany the report home so that parents could see a representative sample of their child's work.

Within specific grades groups of teachers devised their own parent profiles (Figures 7.5 and 7.6). This was a developmental process which ensured that teachers retained ownership of the contents and format of the profiles. Initially these were conceived as a means of building the confidence of parents and of opening up the channels of communic-ation between school and home, and so they had to be constructed in

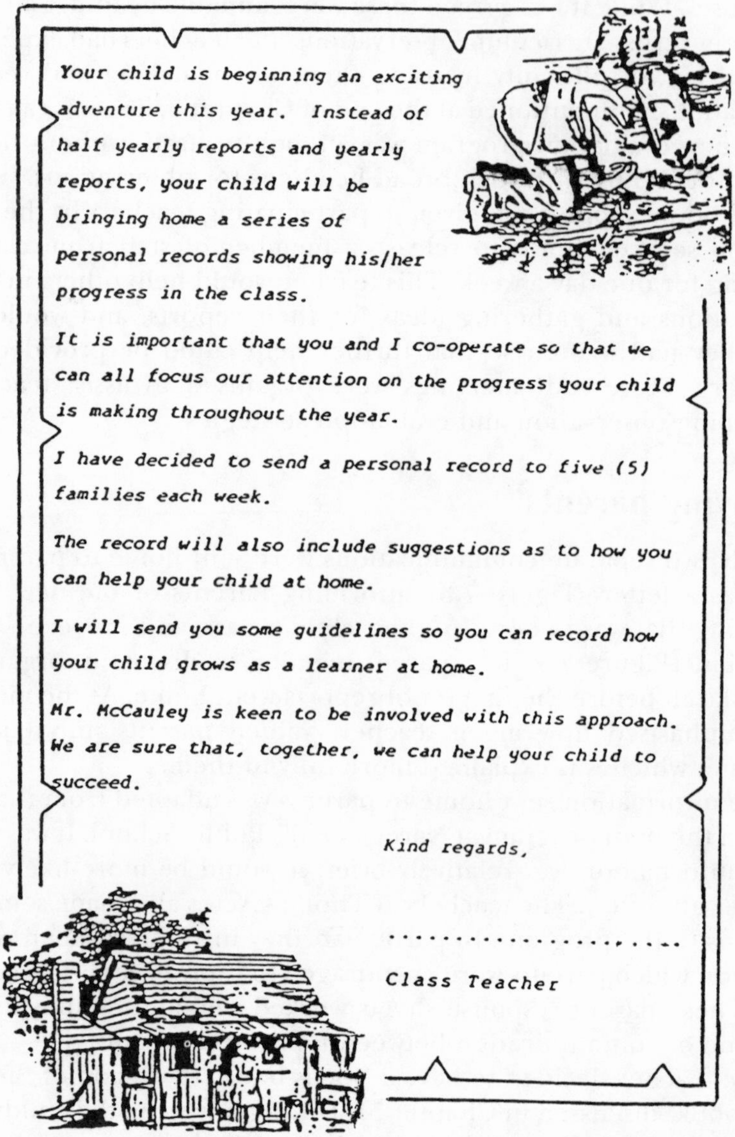

> *Your child is beginning an exciting adventure this year. Instead of half yearly reports and yearly reports, your child will be bringing home a series of personal records showing his/her progress in the class.*
>
> *It is important that you and I co-operate so that we can all focus our attention on the progress your child is making throughout the year.*
>
> *I have decided to send a personal record to five (5) families each week.*
>
> *The record will also include suggestions as to how you can help your child at home.*
>
> *I will send you some guidelines so you can record how your child grows as a learner at home.*
>
> *Mr. McCauley is keen to be involved with this approach. We are sure that, together, we can help your child to succeed.*
>
> *Kind regards,*
>
> *. . . . .*
>
> *Class Teacher*

Figure 7.3

such a way that parents would feel comfortable about filling them in and returning them. Thus some of the early profiles had a 'tick the box' format, though the intention was always that this would later be extended to a more open format encouraging parents to make comments. The procedure was obviously successful as almost all parents returned their profiles.

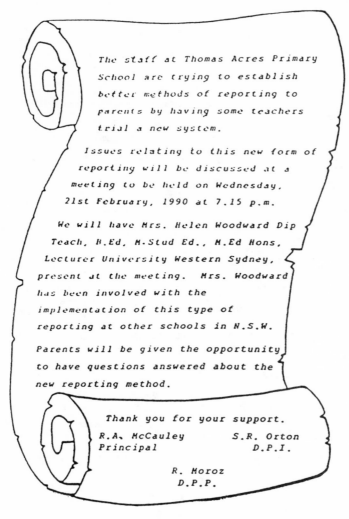

The staff at Thomas Acres Primary
School are trying to establish
better methods of reporting to
parents by having some teachers
trial a new system.

Issues relating to this new form of
reporting will be discussed at a
meeting to be held on Wednesday,
21st February, 1990 at 7.15 p.m.

We will have Mrs. Helen Woodward Dip
Teach, B.Ed, M.Stud Ed., M.Ed Hons,
Lecturer University Western Sydney,
present at the meeting. Mrs. Woodward
has been involved with the
implementation of this type of
reporting at other schools in N.S.W.

Parents will be given the opportunity
to have questions answered about the
new reporting method.

Thank you for your support.
R.A. McCauley   S.R. Orton
Principal   D.P.I.

R. Moroz
D.P.P.

Figure 7.4

Staff development

Thomas Acres also decided to initiate a staff development program
centred on negotiated evaluation. A school grant for curriculum initiatives was successfully applied for. As mentioned earlier, this funded the
release of a teacher for one day a week to support other classroom
teachers implementing the program. It also supplied materials to meet
the demands of a growing school. Since teachers felt a need for more
assistance in focusing their observations, the staff began to develop their

THOMAS ACRES PUBLIC SCHOOL

GRADE 1 PARENT'S REPORT (WRITING)

Child's Name: _____ *Date:* _____

Please comment on your observations of your child's writing at home.

1. *Does your child like to write in his/her leisure time?*

   ☐ *Often* ☐ *Sometimes* ☐ *Never*

   Some of the things my child likes to write about are:

   _____

2. *Does your child like to talk about or display his/her writing?*

   ☐ *Often* ☐ *Sometimes* ☐ *Never*

3. *My child writes in different ways such as (please tick)*

   ☐ *notes and messages* ☐ *diary* ☐ *shopping list*

   ☐ *stories* ☐ *letters* ☐ *factual things*

4. *Does your child feel happy about experimenting with the spelling of new words?*

   ☐ *Usually* ☐ *Sometimes* ☐ *Not really*

5. *What are some of the ways in which your child finds a new word they need for a story?*

   ☐ *asks you* ☐ *asks brother/sister*

   ☐ *looks in book* ☐ *uses a dictionary*

   ☐ *chooses an easier word*

   ☐ *writes the first few letters and checks it out later*

6. *How do you make writing a fun activity at home?*
   (You can use the back of this sheet if you wish)

   _____

   _____

   _____

   Parent's Signature: _____

Figure 7.5

THOMAS ACRES PUBLIC SCHOOL

YEAR 6   CONTINUOUS REPORTING

PARENT'S REPORT ON STUDENT

Child's name: _____   *Date:*_____

As part of the Continuous Reporting procedure at the school Grade 6 teachers would appreciate your comments about your child. Please indicate your observations of your child's reading.

1. *How much encouragements does* _____
    need to read?
    a)   a lot   *b)   some*
    c)   little   *d)   none*

    Comments: _____

    _____

2. *Does* _____ *borrow books from*
    the library?
    a)   a lot   *b)   often*
    c)   sometimes   *d)   occasionally*
    e)   never

    Comments: _____

    _____

3. *What type of books does* _____
    like to read?
    a) comics   *b)   facts (information)*
    c) 'How to Books' (instructional)
    d)   true stories   *e)   fantasy*
    f)   novels   *g)   encyclopaedias*

    Comments: _____

    _____

4. *How do you think* _____ *is*
    progressing as a reader?

    _____

    _____

    Thank you,

    Parent's signature ....

Figure 7.6

repertoire of reading strategies during staff meetings and on pupil-free days, so that they would know better what to look for while they were observing. Thus the program of staff development not only supported the teachers through a period of change but also augmented their professional knowledge.

A variety of proformas for children's reports was used across the school. Some teachers chose to handwrite their reports (Figure 7.7), while others used word processors. Supervising teachers checked each report before it went home. They found that this helped them to track each teacher's development within the program and thus support individual needs more easily.

Half way through the first year of the trial (1990), it became clear that the voluntary nature of the program's implementation was causing difficulties. In a school of this size, coping with two quite different systems was making evaluation and reporting, already a difficult procedure, even more complicated. A decision had to be made about whether or not the program would remain voluntary, and that depended on assessing the relative values of the program under trial and the older reporting system. After a staff review of both systems, 'continuous assessment' was made mandatory within the school for 1991, with the proviso

Principal and staff of Thomas Acres compare different report proformas.

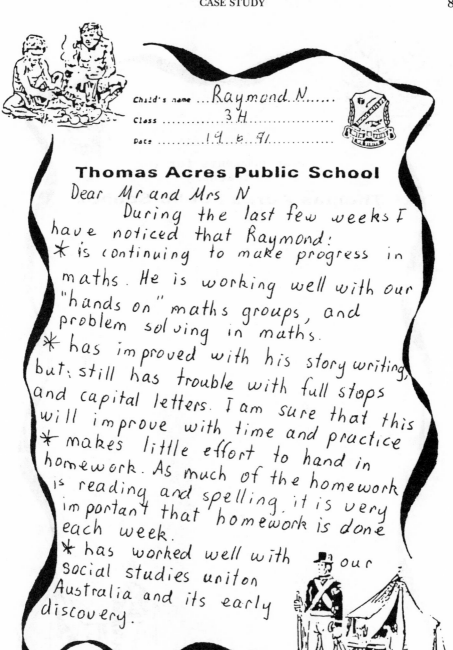

Child's name ...Raymond N......
Class ....3 H................
Date ....19. 6. 91...........

Thomas Acres Public School

Dear Mr and Mrs N

During the last few weeks I have noticed that Raymond:

* is continuing to make progress in maths. He is working well with our "hands on" maths groups, and problem solving in maths.

* has improved with his story writing, but still has trouble with full stops and capital letters. I am sure that this will improve with time and practice

* makes little effort to hand in homework. As much of the homework is reading and spelling it is very important that homework is done each week.

* has worked well with our social studies unit on Australia and its early discovery.

L. a. Hinde

Figure 7.7

CLASS .   NAME   DATE

PARENTS' SAY

(Your comments for the
Teacher)

Thomas Acres Public School

Figure 7.8

that the degree of flexibility and level of staff support built in during 1990 would be retained.

A package was developed in the second half of 1990 to support the program once it became mandatory. Called 'Continuous Reporting', it gave an historical background to the school and the program, an explanation of the program and examples of parent profiles and reports. It was designed to provide assistance to incoming staff as well as existing staff undertaking the program for the first time. There was also a section on data collection, providing some theoretical perspectives and examples of reading strategies to watch for during focused observation.

A parent booklet was devised, as was a strategic plan and time line. Credit for the bulk of the work in these documents must go to the tireless efforts of the school executive: without them the program could not have been implemented successfully.

Current status

Every teacher at Thomas Acres now uses negotiated evaluation in the classroom — with varying degrees of success of course. As with so many educational enterprises, successful implementation depends very much on the understandings and commitment of each teacher. The Principal, Ray McCauley, believes that it would be wise to appoint a coordinator to be responsible for organising and monitoring the program and giving help to those who need it.

During 1992 the program has run without the need for any externally funded support. Further staff meetings have been devoted to consolidating and extending teachers' ideas about negotiated evaluation. One of these meetings introduced teachers to the notion of child-led conferences, and one teacher responded by introducing them immediately.

The degree of parent participation in school activities, while still limited, has improved. The greatest change I have noticed is in the length and quality of the reports emanating from the school and in parents' responses to them. Parents feel their opinions are more valued and in turn value their children's work, because they now know much more about it.

Reports are cumulatively stored in special document holders, which are bought in bulk by the school and then sold at cost to parents when children are enrolled. They are held sucessively by the children's class teachers and are always available to parents on request. Children are presented with them at a special ceremony when they leave the school.

Thomas Acres has hosted several inservice days for teachers from other schools who wanted to find out more about negotiated evaluation.

An interesting feature of these days has been the inclusion of presentations by teachers, children and parents to support the negotiated evaluation model and to provide evidence of the partnerships established within it.

Through the development of their teacher package and their continual input into the education system through inservice days, the staff of Thomas Acres have not only endorsed negotiated evaluation but added to its value and helped to have it recognised as an alternative to more traditional methods of evaluation and reporting. I thank them for their belief in the program and their enthusiasm in developing it.

Epilogue

Now you have sampled the possibilities of negotiated evaluation, the challenge is open for you to set the processes in motion. You may not wish or be able to implement the program in its entirety, but perhaps you can test the water to see how it suits you. If you are adventurous, perhaps you will 'wade in' a little further and try it at, say, a whole grade level — and I know that there will be some of you who will want to 'jump in at the deep end' and fully implement negotiated evaluation in your school.

Testing the water

If you wish to try negotiated evaluation on a small scale, perhaps just in your own classroom, then revisit Chapter 4 (p. 45), where the notion of communication books is explored. The initial ideas developed by Thomas Acres School are also worth investigating. Start small and move slowly, keeping in mind that the children in your care deserve the best you can give them, and that you can only give it to them if you evaluate thoroughly. Negotiated evaluation will help you do just that.

Want to wade?

If you want to implement negotiated evaluation more extensively, perhaps at a whole grade or department level, you will have to do some planning. You will need to help other teachers to develop their understanding of the processes involved, and you may need to give them some practice in focusing, as Thomas Acres School did. You will need also to work with parents, and Chapter 4 should be useful to you here.

Jumping in at the deep end?

So you think the whole school should take on negotiated evaluation. Many schools have made this decision and have implemented it in many different ways. The most important issue is to understand the principles underlying evaluation in general, and negotiated evaluation in particular, as your staff will need a lot of support if the program is to be a success. To do so, you will need not only to revisit this book but also to investigate the references given.

You will best know your staff and how to inservice them, but however you do it, take it slowly. Don't forget that children play a prime role in the process, as do parents, and both should be included wherever possible. Chapters 4 and 5 will help you here.

The never-ending story

This book will never really be finished, because everyone who takes on negotiated evaluation adds another story or another chapter. I am deeply indebted to the many teachers, consultants and friends who have told me the stories related in this book, who have pushed my thinking and ideas into areas where I dared not hope to venture, and who have believed in the idea that has grown to become 'negotiated evaluation'.

References

Anthony, R., T. Johnson, N. Mickelson & A. Preece. 1991. *Evaluating Literacy: A Perspective for Change.* Portsmouth, NH: Heinemann.

Bouffler, C. 1992. "Are Profiles Enough?" In *Literacy Evaluation: Issues and Practicalities,* ed. C. Bouffler. Newtown, NSW: PETA. (Published 1993 by Heinemann, Portsmouth, NH.)

Brown, H. & B. Cambourne. 1987. *Read and Retell: A Strategy for the Whole-Language/Natural Learning Classroom.* Sydney: Methuen. (Published 1989 by Heinemann, Portsmouth, NH.)

Clay, M. 1979. *Reading: The Patterning of Complex Behaviour, 2nd Ed.* Portsmouth, NH: Heinemann. (Later published as *Becoming Literate* by Marie Clay. Portsmouth, NH: Heinemann, 1991.)

Crebbin, W. 1992. "Evaluation: A Political Issue." In *Literacy Evaluation: Issues and Practicalities,* ed. C. Bouffler. Newtown, NSW: PETA. (Published 1993 by Heinemann, Portsmouth, NH.)

Edwards, S. & H. Woodward. 1989. "Negotiating Evaluation." In *Evaluation and Planning for Literacy and Learning: Proceedings of the Tenth Macarthur Reading/Language Symposium,* comp. R. Parker. Sydney: School of Education and Language Studies, University of Western Sydney, Macarthur.

Eisner, E. 1979. *The Educational Imagination: On the Design and Evaluation of School Programs.* New York: Macmillan.

Fryar, R., N. Johnston, & J. Leaker. 1992. "Parents and Assessment." In *Literacy Evaluation: Issues and Practicalities,* ed. C. Bouffler. Newtown, NSW: PETA. (Published 1993 by Heinemann, Portsmouth, NH.)

Goodman, K. 1982. *Language and Literacy: The Selected Writings of Kenneth Goodman.* London: Routledge and Kegan Paul.

Goodman, Y. & C. Burke. 1972. *Reading Miscue Inventory Manual: Procedure for Diagnosis and Evaluation.* New York: Macmillan.

Goodman, Y., D. Watson & C. Burke. 1987. *Reading Miscue Inventory: Alternative Procedures.* Katonah, NY: Richard C. Owen.

Hancock, J. 1992. "Side-by-Side: Responsive Evaluation in a Whole Language Classroom." In *Literacy Evaluation: Issues and Practicalities*, ed. C. Bouffler. Newtown, NSW: PETA. (Published 1993 by Heinemann, Portsmouth, NH.)

Hansen, J. 1992. "Literacy Profiles Emerge." *The Reading Teacher*, April.

Johnston, P. 1992. *Constructive Evaluation of Literate Activity.* New York: Longman.

Newkirk, T. & P. McLure. 1992. *Listening In: Children Talk about Books (and other things).* Portsmouth, NH: Heinemann.

Preece, A. & D. Cowden. 1993. *Young Writers in the Making: Sharing the Process with Parents.* Portsmouth, NH: Heinemann.

Unsworth, L. 1985. "Cloze Procedure Applications to Assessment in Silent Reading." In *Reading: An Australian Perspective*, ed. L. Unsworth. Melbourne: Nelson.

Weaver, C. 1990. *Understanding Whole Language: From Principles to Practice.* Portsmouth, NH: Heinemann.

Western Australia Ministry of Education. 1991. *First Steps.* Perth.

Zessoules, R. & H. Gardiner. 1991. "Authentic Assessment: Beyond the Buzzword." In *Expanding Student Assessment*, eds. Kathe Jervis et al. Alexandria, VA: Association for Supervision and Curriculum Development.